Princeton Theological Monograph Series

Dikran Y. Hadidian

General Editor

33

A CHURCH HISTORIAN'S ODYSSEY
A MEMOIR

A Church
Historian's Odyssey

A Memoir

Horton Davies

PICKWICK PUBLICATIONS
ALLISON PARK, PENNSYLVANIA

Wm. B. EERDMANS PUBLISHING CO.
GRAND RAPIDS, MICHIGAN

Copyright © 1993 by Horton Davies

Published by

Pickwick Publications
4137 Timberlane Drive
Allison Park, PA 15101-2932 USA

and

Wm. B. Eerdmans Publishing Co.
255 Jefferson Avenue S. E.
Grand Rapids, MI 49503

Library of Congress Cataloging-in-Publication Data

Davies, Horton
    A church historian's odyssey : a memoir / Horton Davies.
        p.   cm. -- (Princeton theological monograph series ; 33)

    ISBN 1-55635-018-X (Pickwick Publications)
    ISBN 0-8028-0712-7 (Wm. B. Eerdmans Publishing Co.)

    1. Davies, Horton. 2. Church historians--Great Britain--
Biography. 3. Church historians--United States--Biography.
I. Title. II. Series.
BR139.D38A3 1993
270'.092--dc20
[B]   93-430
                                                                 CIP

For
my Children
and Grandchildren

CONTENTS

PREFATORY NOTE

This book is not an autobiography, but a memoir. It says at least as much about my social, geographical and historical contexts as about myself. In this way I hoped to avoid the dangers in Carlyle's warning: "A well-written life is almost as rare as a well-spent one." I also trust that the readers will glimpse some sense that, in the words of John Gay: "Variety's the source of joy below."

What *is* the variety? It is the multitude of recollections reported with affection. It is a record of over seventy years spent on the Continents of Europe, Africa, and North America, with comparisons of the modes and values of life in Scotland, England, the Eastern Cape Province of South Africa and the United States, with shorter stays in Wales, France, Germany, Holland, Canada and Israel. It is also an account of the vicissitudes of two careers as a Protestant Minister of Religion and as a University teacher at Rhodes University in Grahamstown, South Africa, Oxford and Princeton. It also recalls the start of a lively retirement. It records challenges and attempts to deal with them, my writings and paintings, my family and friends, my students and my colleagues and their publications and varied careers. The writing is illustrated by narratives, interviews, scenic descriptions, many amusing anecdotes, and with light verse and worse!

Horton Davies
Princeton, New Jersey, U.S.A
Summer 1992

UPBRINGING AND EDUCATION

A postman handing me my mail in a Vermont village and seeing the names on the envelope, "Daniel Timothy Horton Marlais Davies" observed, "When your folks baptized you they sure gave you a set of goofers." I agreed with him and since undergraduate days I used only "Horton Davies." But the names tell a story. Daniel was my paternal grandfather, a Carmarthenshire farmer in central Wales, while Timothy, my maternal grandfather, was a sea captain whose children were born at three and a half year intervals, since his ship "The West Lothian" took three years to sail from Ardrossan, Scotland to the major ports of North and South America, requiring him to round Cape Horn. I have one treasured souvenir showing him and his four-masted ship with the inscription: "Captain Timothy Davies, the Welsh Consul, the first to support the opposition." This meant that at Buenos Aires the multiple foreign ships were led by him in refusing the irrational conditions imposed by Custom officials. The name "Horton" was chosen by my father because of his admiration for the Revd. Robert Forman Horton, the first Congregationalist since the days of Cromwell to be elected to a Fellowship at Oxford University, at New College, who later became minister of Hampstead Garden Free Church, the most important Congregational Church in London after the City Temple. My father, a Welsh Congregational Minister, needing a pseudonym for his entries in the poetry competitions of the National Eisteddfod, chose the French name "Marlais" because a river near his home in Llansadwrn had been given this name by the French Protestant refugees who had escaped there from seventeenth century Catholic persecution.

As for the surname Davies, it was both my father's and my mother's before her marriage, and is as common in Wales as is Smith in England, but is much appreciated because the patron saint of Wales was St. David.

My first three years were spent in Wales in Cwmavon, near Port Talbot in Glamorganshire, an area which boasted the birth of the actor, Richard Burton. Cwmavon was a mining village and rejoiced that its minister was a convinced Christian Socialist, and even tried to persuade him to leave the ministry for a political career. My mother was a secondary school teacher and one of the earliest graduates of Aberystwyth University College of the University of Wales and had concentrated on French language and literature. She died when I was nine, and my brother Dorian only three. Photographs of her show a face of lively compassion and brightly colored clothing with tricolor hats. After Cwmavon my father accepted a call to Providence Congregational Church, Middleton, near Manchester where he remained from 1919 to 1934. Then he went to George Square Congregational Church in Greenock until 1939, when he became minister of the Avenue Congregational Church, Southampton, a highly prestigious appointment, for his predecessor, Stanley Herbert, had left Southampton to become minister of the Hampstead Garden Suburb Free Church in London.

My father was a handsome and popular man, usually elegantly dressed, and a considerable athlete. He held the Cardiff University high jump record for several years, discovering this capacity thanks to a bull on the family farm chasing him, and forcing him to jump a fence that was six feet high to escape. He once did a standing jump for me in the back garden in Middleton, Manchester higher than four feet. I am still astonished that a Nonconformist minister, who had never played golf in all his years in Wales should have become captain of the Manchester Golf Club, as he did in the 1920's. He was also a hunter of rabbits and foxes—one of the latter graced the back of our living room settee.

His real distinction was as a preacher in Welsh and when in England he often returned to Wales for the different preaching festivals that most Welsh churches held on weeknights. It was a delight to me to be told by the Oxford University Professor of Celtic, Idris L. Foster, when dining at the high table at Jesus College in 1954, that David Marlais Davies was the most eloquent preacher he had ever heard. I, of course, heard him preach many times in English and what I remember as outstanding was his sonorous and mellifluous voice that could declaim with indignation and whisper in compassion, his memorable illustrations, and his psychological analyses, all of which held the attention of his congregations enthralled. It was only fitting that after his years in Manchester, and in Greenock on the West Coast of Scotland, that his final most important ministry should have been at the distinguished and most important Free Church in Southampton, the Avenue Congregational Church. He began there the day the Second World War broke out and remained throughout the blitz. He was proud to be a free Church chaplain at the Southampton docks which historically welcomed the Mayflower Pilgrims and from which the vast Cunarders left to cross the Atlantic and bring back American allies. His courage in these years of bombing was entirely typical of him. So when a government committee was appointed to determine which of the bombed out churches in the southern region were to be rebuilt, with the Anglican Bishop of Winchester as Chairman, and the Roman Catholic Bishop of Portsmouth as Treasurer, father was appointed Secretary for he had remained at his dangerous post throughout the war years.

Two stepmothers took my mother's place during my youth, the first found me unattractive since I was usually bending down over the kitchen fire and reading books, with my tie askew and socks down at my ankles. Her stay as stepmother was unexpectedly brief because she died giving birth to twin girls, only one of whom survived, Gloria, my half-sister. She, a highly capable nurse and school teacher and her economist husband, Michael Scott, have spent an interesting career under the aegis of U.N.E.S.C.O. in faraway countries such as Romania, Sri Lanka, Tanganyika, and the Cayman Islands. I have one memory, unerasable, which happily she does not share—that of seeing her mother in her wide coffin with the pathetic dead twin baby beside her.

Happily for my father, his third marriage was one of legendary happiness, and a real mother could not have been kinder to Gloria, Dorian, and myself. But it was Gloria's mother that led my brother and myself being sent out of the house to a boarding school. As we children bothered her, my father sent us away to Silcoates School, near Wakefield, Yorkshire. Here Dorian at eight years of age was immensely popular as the youngest boy in the school, whereas I, more retired by nature, found it less attractive. Silcoates was a private school founded for sons of Congregational ministers and foreign missionaries of the London Missionary Society. Its most famous Victorian alumnus was W. T. Stead, the editor first of the *Pall Mall Gazette*, an evening paper, and later of the influential monthly magazine, *The Review of Reviews*. He has been described as "the bravest and most brilliant of all English journalists." A more recent alumnus was Dr. Will Moore, Professor and Fellow of St. John's College, Oxford, a senior editor of *The Modern Language Review*, and Chairman of the Board of Governors of Mansfield College, Oxford, who was to prove a good friend to me. Its most famous alumnus in the present century is the medical missionary, Dr. Eric Liddell, the runner in the film, *Chariots of Fire*. The school is now coeducational and maintains a high reputation in the north of England.

Three incidents at the school remain vivid in my memory. The first was my introduction to the Rawson House dormitory. All the new boys, like myself, were told to stand in line in their pyjamas, while the mats were lined up in a straight path between the two sets of beds. Each of us was told to carry his chamber pot, then to kneel down, when the chamber pot was clamped on his head and his rear end was walloped with the knotted towels of the senior boys. It was a more frightening initiation than a fierce or hurtful one.

My second memory was volunteering to creep out of the dormitory one night, to walk down the stairs past the housemaster's bedroom, and enter the lounge of the masters there to copy the list of the grades of the seniors in the house dormitory and, as proof that I had done this, to stop the clock on the mantel-piece with tobacco from a communal tobacco jar. This was done with some anxiety followed by relief.

The third incident was the visit of the renowned Yorkshire Wanderers Rugby team to play the school's first fifteen on which I was a mere reserve. The Wanderers were one man short and unathletic I played on "their" team, which demolished the school team by 82 points to 5, and of the massive total I scored an easy try (or touchdown) to the envy or shame of my schoolmates.

On the whole life at the school was admirable and the Headmaster, Sydney H. Moore, was a benevolent tyrant with a gift for teaching modern languages, an admirable cricket coach, and a convinced Protestant who had dared to sell Bibles in Catholic Spain, whose bullet-damaged arm was testimony of it. He used to convene the students of the upper forms in a large hall and once a week read at dictation speed passages from French literature. He subtracted a point for every mistake in the *Dictée* and, since the top mark was 20, most of the class had minus marks. Eventually one reached 14 or 16. The result was that the school gained an amazing number of certificates for high competence in French from *La Société des Professeurs Français en Angleterre* at a standard at least equivalent to first year French at the university level. Although I left school at sixteen in the upper fifth form, instead of the usual sixth, I managed to gain two prizes: the school Shakespeare Prize and the school Hymnlore Prize, and a Phoenix Leaving Scholarship tenable at a university. Those prizes were prophecies of my future development, since I took an Honours English M.A. at the University of Edinburgh, and followed it with a B.D. with Highest Honours in Systematic Theology, gaining a Gunning Prize in Divinity. For years my primary theological interest was in the historical development of Christian worship and my Oxford doctorate was titled, *The Worship of the English Puritans* which was published by the Dacre Press, and many years later I wrote an ecumenical history of worship in England in five volumes, published by the Presses of the Universities of Princeton and Oxford. I continued to delight in reading English literature all my life, regularly taught a course on Religion and Literature at Princeton University, and even wrote a book entitled, *Catching the Conscience* which correlated theology with literature.

Throughout my youth I was firmly disciplined in religious knowledge and devotion. This meant attending services each Sunday at 10:30 a.m. and 6:30 p.m. and Sunday School at 9:00 a.m. and 3:00 p.m., not forgetting a weeknight service each Wednesday at 7:30 p.m. It is not surprizing that having a father whom I admired greatly I thought of no other vocation than that of becoming a Congregational minister. This was strengthened by a contrasting experience. When I left school at sixteen I was sent to work in a dye factory—the Calico Printers at Rhodes—for the best part of a year. I began for the first two weeks doing nothing but training my hands to feed cotton into rollers which took them through various colors. Ever since that experience I have sympathized with factory workers who do repetitive, mind battering jobs for a living. After those two weeks I moved into the chemistry laboratory to help with the mixing of the colors. I still recall the shock of being introduced to one color-mixer with the words "Young man, shake hands with a murderer." The story was, as I later discovered, that this man, a soldier in the First World War, had unexpectedly returned home on leave to find a neighbor in bed with his wife. Immediately he took out his revolver and shot the intruder!

When my year was almost completed, I went to stay for three weeks in Wallasey near Liverpool with my father's eldest sister, Aunt Olwen and her husband, who owned and managed a combined barber's shop and candy store. I had three weeks in which to learn Hellenistic Greek from scratch for the interpretation of the New Testament for an examination to admit me to theological training. It was agony during the day but a delight in the evenings because, as the shop posted advertisements of all the local movie houses, I could go to a different film free almost every night. At the end of three weeks I travelled to Bradford, Yorkshire to The Yorkshire United Independent College to be examined as a candidate for theological training. All matriculants were sent by this college to Edinburgh University on scholarships for three or four years, and I was sucessful. Thereafter I spent four years at this University taking the Honours English degree, under the supervision of two superb Heads of the English Department, Professor Sir Herbert Grierson and Professor J. Dover Wilson. The first was a great authority on two very different Christians, John Donne, young rake and converted Dean of St. Paul's Cathedral, London, in the seventeenth century and Sir Walter Scott, the romantic novelist of nineteenth century Scotland. Professor Dover Wilson was the editor of the distinguished Cambridge University edition of the plays of Shakespeare. In my first year at Edinburgh, to my great surprise, I gained the English medal in a large class of over a hundred and twenty students and I remember how disappointed I was when the medal was neither gold nor silver, but only bronze.

Far more enjoyable was playing two roles in the University Dramatic Club, which was organized and coached by I. A. Gordon, Lecturer in English, who later had a distinguished career in New Zealand. My first role was the minor part of the foolish and bibulous knight, Sir Andrew Aguecheek, in Shakespeare's *Twelfth Night*. In the following year I was cast as the Cardinal in Webster's *The Duchess of Malfi*, a Prince of the Church who went mad. I

thoroughly enjoyed the capers that his idiocy required me
to make, although a review of the play observed that I
showed singularly little dignity for a Cardinal. A high point
of these four years was the opportunity to hear the great Albert Schweitzer deliver the Gifford Lectures, without a note
in perfect English, and to listen to him in the Usher Hall
playing several of Bach's Fugues and Preludes on the organ. One was simply staggered that so fine a theologian
who had written the famous *The Quest for the Historical
Jesus*, and was an outstanding musician, had given all this
up to study for a medical degree in order to go to the malar-
ia-infested village of Lambaréné in French West Africa to
dedicate his life to the lepers. The only originality I demon-
strated during my undergraduate years was to publish in
The Student under the pseudonym "Notroh"—my first
name reversed—a set of five "Profane Epitaphs" lampoon-
ing some of the most famous personalities of the middle
nineteen thirties. Here they are:

She lies not here: MAE'S gone WEST
To be the Devil's wittiest guest;
But she with tactful grace left word:
"Come down and see me sometime, Lord."

When MUSSOLINI went to Heaven,
He took the place by storm;
He bombarded all the angels
And signed a non-agression form!

On Styx's side lies BERNARD SHAW,
Who always was a rebel;
Now he's got an immortal change
To be the only pebble...

Down in Hell they're working overtime,
But see old Satan grinning through the grime;
Have you heard his latest joke?
BALDWIN'S just gone up in smoke!

BROADCASTING FROM HEAVEN

"We're SCOTT and BLACK you now hear sing, We've
been forced down here with a crumpled wing.
From Earth to Heaven within a day!
We wonder what the Aero Club will say?"

After completing the M.A. degree *Magna cum
laude* (not Maxima) in 1937, coming for three years down
to Bradford to a small theological college seemed an anti-
climax. But there were also compensations. One great benefit was provided every Friday afternoon in the Sermon
Class in which each of us had to preach and have our sermons criticized by both the professors and the students. I
was deeply impressed by the categories which we were required to use in evaluating the sermons we heard, and it influenced me for life. Each sermon was examined for its fidelity to Scripture, for its clarity of meaning and the ease of
remembering its structure, for the relevance and vitality of
its illustrations, for its practical benefits, and, finally, for
the audibility and gestures of the preacher. These set high
standards both theologically and rhetorically, and it was
good to be reminded to live up to them.

Another compensation was at last to be able to use
the practical training for the ministry. At the Congregational Church of Kipping Thornton near Bradford, I was for
two years able to share the student ministry with George
Clamp, a former professional footballer now training with
me. We got on famously together. He had a marvellous
sense of humor and was a warm and compassionate personality who related well with everybody. His visits to the sick
or unhappy were widely remembered, and his sermons
were down-to-earth practical homilies. My own sermons
were nearly always a series of doctrinal expositions and
were perhaps occasionally over long. I remember a certain
Alderman (as they called senior local city councillors) who
sat in the furthest seat away from the pulpit under the gallery. When my sermon had reached 20 minutes, he would

stand up holding his hat in one hand and a walking stick in
the other, a provocative signal to me to finish, which I always pretended not to see !

During my seminary days in Bradford I received
unusually high standard lecturing in New Testament Studies from Professor J. C. Ormerod who later taught at Mansfield College, in Church History from the Principal Ernest
J. Price, and in Systematic Theology from Hubert Cunliffe-
Jones who afterwards became the first Professor of Theology to be appointed by Manchester University. This Australian was the living embodiment of genuine Christianity, fair
to all ecumenical viewpoints and thinkers, free of all fad-
dishness, yet always open to new insights and ever encouraging. He it was who introduced me to the depth and
breadth of the great North African Saint Augustine, and encouraged me to go on to Oxford University, and to his old
theological college there, Mansfield. In the meantime I had
become engaged to my future first wife, Brenda Mary Deakin, whose virtues had been advertised to me by a close
friend, George Cleaves, who had seen her the year before I
did and heard her play the piano. I, too, saw her at the
grand piano in Westhill Training College, Birmingham,
dressed in a long white robe. I came, I saw, I *was* con-
quered by this Froebel teacher-in-training.

While at Mansfield College, Oxford, I listened to
the lively lectures of Professor A. M. Hunter on the New
Testament, Professor C. J. Cadoux on Early Church History, Principal Wheeler Robinson on the Old Testament, and
Professor Nathaniel Micklem on those great theologians,
St. Thomas Aquinas and Peter Taylor Forsyth. In those
years a theological battle went on in the College between
the liberals, led by Cadoux the Vice-Principal whom I admired for his courage and consistency as a pacifist, and
Micklem who was in the *avant-garde* of the Neo-Orthodox,
an important anti-liberal theology most famously defended
and expounded by Karl Barth, the Swiss theologian who
had while in Germany challenged the theologians who
compromised with Hitler. Micklem was a man of unusual

charm and plentiful wit and wisdom, and he and Archbishop William Temple were the only clergymen in England whose eloquence caused them as undergraduates to be chosen Presidents of the Oxford Union, where several politicians of distinction, including cabinet ministers, made their first speeches. Once again, I had been most fortunate in my mentors.

On reaching Oxford I had hoped to undertake a research degree. There were two such, the humbler B. Litt. and the more advanced, the D. Phil. Since I made it clear that my topic would be the development of the Puritan tradition in worship I was sent to the university lecturer in liturgiology, the Revd. Edmund Cradock Ratcliff, Fellow and Chaplain of the Queen's College. When I met him he told me he knew nothing about Puritan worship, but that I was welcome to his lectures on Roman Catholic and Anglican worship. This seemed a slap in the face, with its implication that my topic was not worth studying. But, in fact, these lectures taught me to be fair to the alternative forms of worship and I was fortunate to be able in tutorials with him to present each fortnight a chapter of my proposed dissertation. Before the first term was over he wrote a letter to the Faculty of Theology petitioning for my status to be changed from that of a B. Litt. to a D. Phil. student. I found it to be true that one's tutor at Oxford was to be a lifelong friend, even though he was an Anglo-Catholic and I a Dissenter. He it was, in fact, who sent my doctoral dissertation to a High Anglican publishing house, The Dacre Press of Westminster, which was in the process of publishing one of the greatest works of liturgiology of the twentieth century, namely, Dom Gregory Dix's *The Shape of the Liturgy* which appeared in 1946. Here I met the stimulating Anglican Benedictine author and because of the wartime shortage of paper waited another two years before my dissertation was published. Another indication of the kindness of Ratcliff was his invitation, as Regius Professor of Divinity at Cambridge University to me to preach the official University Sermon on Ascension Day in 1961.

Comparing my university experiences at Edinburgh and Oxford, as well as my subsequent ones of teaching in Rhodes University in South Africa and at Princeton University in the United States, has forced me to ask why the ancient universities of Oxford and Cambridge in England have pre-eminence over even the older universities in Scotland or the more modern universities throughout Britain or in the Dominions and Colonies? (Later I shall consider the strengths of the Ivy League universities and the famous state universities of the U.S.A.) I might mention in passing that the quality of universities is not merely an academic matter. The entire population benefits or loses by the strength or weakness of universities. The quality of physicians, lawyers, ministers of religion, headmasters and headmistresses in local secondary schools, and of leading politicians and scientists, is determined by the universities they attend as well as by their own efforts.

What, then, did I find distinctive about Oxford University? To begin with, it had tradition going back to the Middle Ages. For example, Christ Church, the largest College, was founded by Cardinal Wolsey, and when an undergraduate dines in its vast hall he is confronted by oil-paintings of the past famous members of the College, including several Prime Ministers of England, and not less important, a portrait of John Wesley. The same undergraduate has only to cross the Great Quadrangle to the rooms in which a clerical and mathematical don of the Victorian age, Lewis Carrol, wrote the immortal *Alice in Wonderland*. The chapel of this College is the Cathedral of Oxford. What an inspiration such scenes are to successively privileged generations of undergraduates !

Oxford University is a place where wit is appreciated and which punctuates both lectures and conversations in the senior common rooms. In the middle nineteen-fifties, when the Canadian Rhodes Scholar, Lowe, was the Head or Dean of Christ Church, he was also Vice-Chancellor of the University of Oxford and had decided to fly to a conference in Torquay in a helicopter. Many of the undergraduates met him on his return all singing with great gusto the echo of the hymn: "Lo[we] he comes with clouds descending!"

Besides tradition, Oxford and Cambridge have a remarkable tutorial system. This is possible partly because in addition to university professors, readers, and lecturers receiving university emoluments, each separate College also has its tutorial fellows who are responsible for academic tuition as well as for personal advice to the undergraduates. It is an immense privilege to be able to read one's essays at frequent intervals, often fortnightly, each term to different experts in the field and to receive their criticisms and encouragements. Thus, the endowments of the ages (needing to be replenished in current days) with the superb modern donations of Cecil Rhodes, Viscount Nuffield and Sir John Templeton (American Rhodes Scholar) mean that the ancient universities attract distinguished teachers as well as distinguished undergraduate and postgraduate students.

For example, when in the mid-fifties I lectured at Oxford, there were 43 members of the Faculty of Theology compared with three full-time and two parttime teachers in the Faculty of Divinity at Rhodes University, South Africa. Each student therefore receives fuller attention in a larger variety of sub-disciplines in his or her field. Furthermore, each university teacher also benefits because he or she has ample time and superb research facilities for books and experimentation.

The third advantage Oxford and Cambridge have is keen competition. No intending student who has not obtained either a degree from another university, or the equivalent of the Higher School Certificate (two years beyond matriculation or university entrance standard) is able to enter the ancient universities. Furthermore, Oxford and Cambridge do not readily tolerate failures, because there are good men and women waiting to enter, and the drones must not keep them out. Only keen students reach Oxford and Cambridge and generally they stay keen.

The terms are short, only eight weeks in duration, with a briefer summer term, and students are recommended to attend relevant lectures, but are not coerced, with the exception of the required essay for their tutors. The rest of the time is their own and they are offered a feast of intellectual fare. They may choose to enter debates at the Oxford Union where they may be seen by many of the great politicians of the future and occasionally, as guests, Cabinet Ministers of the day. If they choose they can attend either of the two theatres, and hear the leading preachers of England at St. Mary's Church, where John Henry Newman was once the admired Vicar. There are also innumerable debating societies and athletic opportunities with the chance to earn a "blue" at rowing, rugby, soccer, hockey, cricket, or other sports. During the three years of an undergraduate's life, he is required to sit exams at the end of his first year, and a whole week's examinations of considerable stiffness at the end of his third year, in which his future is almost guaranteed educationally if he is awarded a First Class Honours degree. A small number only are awarded for brilliance and originality as well as erudition.

To indicate the extraordinary variety of interesting encounters possible at Oxford, during a single fortnight in 1954, I noted that the Archbishop of Canterbury preached at St. Mary's, the "red dean" of Canterbury addressed the Socialist Society, the Liberal leader, Mr. Clement Davies, addressed the Liberal Society, and Shaw's *Pygmalion* was playing at the Playhouse. You could also have heard Sir Maurice Powicke lecturing on the contribution of Bishop Grosseteste to medieval philosophical and scientific thought, and Mr. Kirkwood, a visitor from Natal University, South Africa, speaking in the Town Hall on "Race Problems in South Africa", and Professor Waterhouse analyzing painting in the High Renaissance, and Principal Vincent Taylor lecturing on Christ in the New Testament. Here indeed was God's plenty. The convenient closeness of Oxford and Cambridge to London makes such a plethora of important visitors willing to come to be warmly received.

This account may seem too good to be true, more utopian than realistic. I should add, greatly daring, that I preferred the man-to-man approach of South African and

American students to their teachers, to the deferential delicacy of the standard Oxford contact. Secondly, I have a suspicion that snobbery and certainly complacency flourish in Oxon-Cantab. products. Thirdly, while tradition can certainly be a guide, it can also degenerate into a chain. In the theological faculty in my time the backward look was so very pronounced—that to lecture, as I did on the Reformation, seemed almost indecently recent, whereas the approved alternative periods were those of the Early Church and the Middle Ages. But how could undergraduates learn about either the extraordinary nineteenth and twentieth century expansion of Christianity or the cheering development of the Ecumenical Movement? Yet for all my questioning of the defects of Oxford and Cambridge, I cannot doubt their pre-eminence in Britain or the stimulus they provide for their students from so many countries worldwide.

I cannot end this chapter without an expression of gratitude for those who were my friends at school, university and theological college, as well as to the closest member of my family in the early years. My earliest friend, who accompanied me on the two trams that took us from Middleton to the North Manchester Grammar School, and from whose unroofed tops, we catapulted tram tickets at our betters entering or leaving the trams below, was Rodney Hilton. Little did either of us then guess that we should be professors or historians. He became at Birmingham University a distinguished medieval social historian of a leftish stripe and ended his career there as Director of the Institute of Advanced Research in the Humanities. My closest friend at Edinburgh and Bradford was the sensitive and loyal George Cleaves, afterwards a clergyman in England and a secondary school teacher of divinity, and a man in love with classical music. At Oxford a close friend was Philip Lee-Woolf, a good scholar, lively debater, and popular member of the College, who after a successful ministy at the famous Carr's Lane Congregational Church in Birmingham led the ecumenical Student Christian Movement of Great Britain.

If the impression has been given that my formative years were impecunious and devoted only to cramming for examinations, this is a misrepresentation. I was, indeed, always short of money, but for my years at Edinburgh University, apart from the scholarships that sustained me, I was able to earn a pittance of one pound five shillings sterling per week (about six American dollars equivalent at that time) as an assistant purser on the Clyde steamers that sailed all day from Gourock or Greenock to the island of Arran or to Inveraray through the Kyles of Bute—beautiful coastal trips on the West coast of Scotland. Often we were also required to go on evening cruises as well that ended near midnight, but this life was made delightful by two circumstances. Each day one of the courses of the lunch included fresh Loch Fyne salmon, and the assistant pursers were the favorites of the local schoolgirls who bought season tickets to spend the summer with them!

Even before these sailing days as an undergraduate, I had spent joyful holidays with my Welsh aunts at Aberayron in Cardiganshire and my grandmother in Llansadwrn in Carmarthenshire. The combination of two weeks at the seaside paddling and fishing in pools, and helping to feed the animals on the inland farm for a third or fourth week was always a source of joy. And one year I was able to spend the time with Ian Leitch, a Greenock friend, and Glasgow undergraduate, who settled in his native town as a much honored physician. I realize again how fortunate I was in my relations and my friends and my teachers far more than I deserved. One treasured playmate of the early summer was my cousin Trefor Wyn in Llanwrda near Llansadwrn who was a most amusing, daring, and mischievous boy, who drove trucks illegally when he was only twelve years of age. I remember him challenging his all-too-tolerant father one day by climbing up the monkey-puzzle tree (so symbolically right) in front of the house by taunting him as he returned after a hard day's work as organiser of a major District of the Cooperative Wholesale Society. Who would have predicted that he would become a valuable Alderman of the County Council of Carmarthenshire?

2

MINISTER OF A SOUTH LONDON CHURCH

1942 was an *annus mirabilis*. I left Oxford, was married to Brenda Mary Deakin in Birmingham, and ordinand to the ministry of the Word and Sacraments at the Congregational Church (now the United Reformed Church since the English Presbyterians and Congregationalists united) of Wallington and Carshalton in Surrey. The towns were southern suburbs of London and adjacent to Croydon airport, which endangered their location during the aerial bombardment of the Second World War, but that is another story.

The service of ordination was immensely important for me. It was usual to have present the Moderator (approximately equivalent to a Bishop) and two other ministers who would remind the minister-to-be of his sacred duties, and members of the church of their responsibilities under Christ to support the minister. The "Charge" to the ordinand was delivered by Principal Nathaniel Micklem, D.D., LL.D., the Head of my Oxford College, Mansfield, and the "Charge" to the church by my father, the Revd. Dr. D. Marlais Davies, Minister of the Avenue Congregational Church, Southampton. These "Charges" made vividly clear the significant covenantal nature of the cooperation of minister and people. The heart of the service was, however, the prayer for the descent of the Holy Spirit upon the one to be ordained to sanctify him for the ministry. This was offered by the Moderator of the London Congregational Churches, while the other ministers present laid their hands on my head as the petition was made. Significantly, however, two laymen, the president of the board of local deacons and the secretary, Messrs. Penry Edwards and Harold Ireland, also laid their hands on me. This was a vivid way of expressing the priesthood of all believers. It emphasized the strongly democratic character of Congregationalism, which transplanted their proto-Puritan ancestors from Plymouth in England to Plymouth Rock in Massachusetts in the Mayflower, that seed-bed of American democracy. The presence of College colleagues, relatives, and friends made the solemn event a personal delight.

Even as I write I am amazed that a lively London church was willing in the throes of war to invite a twenty-four year old student to be their minister, especially when I think of the responsibilities exercised by three of the deacons on the board which advised me. Penry Edwards was principal officer responsible for the supervision of the overseas branches of the National Provincial Bank, one of the flve largest banks in Britain. His associates as deacons were Walter Holman, who had been President of the British Association of Incorporated Accountants, and Harold Ireland, No. 2 in the largest building society in England, the Abbey National. Never did they suggest that I was immature!

I had, however, been prepared for this responsibility by three student pastorates amongst the hard-headed Yorkshire folk in two years at Thornton and a summer in Halifax, and among the smoother Southerners in a summer pastorate in Southampton, punctuated by fire bombs. I had also had opportunities to preach at many different churches on single Sundays in Scotland as well as in England. The congregations were marvellously encouraging for a learner.

During my three and a half years in Wallington I introduced four changes in the running of the church. First, while according to Nonconformist practice we did not use a liturgy, yet I varied the prayers to avoid becoming stereotyped, and interjected spoken responses so that the congregation was involved in more than silent prayer. I increased the frequency of the services of the Lord's Supper or Holy Communion, a major additional change. Instead of being held at monthly intervals, they became fortnightly, in the morning service on the first Sunday of the month, and in the evening on the third Sunday of the month. Also, I preached Communion sermons on these occasions, stressing the great privilege of attending. Although I could not in conscience say: "All are welcome" because this would imply the lack of any need of instruction in the meaning of the chief sacrament, I did not want anyone to stay away by raising the barriers of solemnity. For this purpose I made the following invitation in the first part of the service: "Members of any branch of Christ's Church are welcome at Christ's Table."

Before introducing these changes, I divided the membership of the church into four adjacent areas and we met in each of them once every month for a series of addresses and discussions on the meaning of worship, which led to the composition of my book, *Christian Worship: Its Making and Meaning* published conveniently by the Religious Education Press of Wallington, Surrey.

The fourth change was most radical. I believed in the importance of continuity in instruction and that meant preaching several series of sermons. An obvious choice was to preach a series on the Apostles' Creed as a convenient summary of Christian doctrine, which I did.

I suppose that one of the biggest problems a preacher faces is the ever recurrent question: What shall I preach on next? It was no problem for the Puritan divines who, before the advent of Biblical Criticism, believed in the full inspiration of the Holy Spirit in the entire Bible. So they simply went on expounding one chapter after another until they had explained the spiritual meaning of the entire New Testament, following that with a substantial portion of the Old Testament which.they saw as anticipating and pointing forward to the New Testament. Inevitably in my time, it was recognized that the Bible in its different parts had varying degrees of inspiration. The ensuing danger was that the preacher would preach on texts or passages of Holy Writ that made an immediate appeal to him because of their recording of an important event, their instant relevance, or their attractive literary form as narrative, parable, allegory

or apothegm. One certain way of trying to evade such
temptations was to take a central theological theme in its
many aspects and to expound that in depth and detail.

For example, I preached a series of sermons on the
Crucifixion as an event and illustrated its meaning then and
now by the responses to it. The title, which was advertised
boldly outside the church for passers by to see clearly, was
CROSS-EXAMINATION, and several different witnesses
were considered. I tried to make their presence as vivid as
possible. I can give as an example my treatment of the first
witness, Mary the Mother of Jesus, recorded by the Gospel
of John 19:25, as follows: "Standing by the cross of Jesus,
His mother . . . " The sermon began:

> I summon Mary as the first witness of the Crucifixion.
> Look at her carefully: but do not pry too closely. She has
> borne the weight of some fifty tragic years on her slender
> shoulders. Her hands worn thin with toil are clasped me-
> chanically in prayer. Her lips are mute, but her stifled sobs
> speak thoughts that are deeper than tears. The beloved dis-
> ciple has his right arm on her shoulder–but her world is tot-
> tering: no hand can arrest its crashing momentum. What
> are her thoughts?

Using my imagination, I assumed that the first reaction was the sense of sheer futility of the Cross, and the second the sheer folly of it and its appalling waste consequent
on Christ's verbal attacks on the Scribes and Pharisees of
Jerusalem. Then came the third reaction, very late. Perhaps
Jesus was right. His accusers were mistaken: he was never
a blasphemer. As for the superscription on the Cross that
He claimed to be King of the Jews, this too was mistaken
for he had always refused to be a popular political leader.
Then I continued:

> Her mind flashed back to the scrolls of the prophecies of
> Isaiah they had at home and how Jesus was always reading
> them, and one in particular was more thumbed than the
> rest. How strange it seemed that her son, sparkling with

life in those far-off days, should be reading the saddest of all passages in the Hebrew Scriptures: "He was despised and rejected of men"–that was the passage. "He is despised and rejected among men." The realization had dawned: Jesus is the Suffering Servant–God's Messiah. He is right! A brilliant dawn two days later was to turn the possibility into a certainty. But it was more than she had dared to hope for aloud standing beside the Cross.

And the meaning for modern Maries and Josephs struck by tragedies is to learn the obedience of faith, for in the words of a modern theologian, "The Incarnation began when Mary said, 'Into Thy hands I commend my body,' and ended when Jesus said, 'Into thy hands I commend my spirit.'" I ended with the following words:

Those who keep tryst with God through the dark night of trial shall see the clouds of darkness hurrying before the golden chariots of Easter dawn. Nothing can separate us from the love of God in Jesus Christ our Lord. Nothing.

This example of a greatly condensed and summarized sermon is merely an illustration of the vividness of narrative, the psychological relevance, and the sympathy required of all preachers to gain and to hold the attention of a congregation.

A similar technique was employed in the cross-examination of Judas Iscariot, Caiaphas, King Herod the Fox, Pontius Pilate, Joseph of Arimathea the City Councillor, and the Soldier, totalling seven witnesses in all, and others, such as Peter, could have been added to the number for Mark 14:50 records "all the disciples forsook him and fled."

Another series, this time of six sermons, was entitled, CHRISTIAN CONVICTIONS. This began with "The Divine Architect: God the Creator" and continued with "The Incarnation: God stooping to conquer"; "The Atonement as the Divine Blood-Transfusion"; "The Resurrection:

Terminus becoming Tunnel"; "the Great Judgement at History's End"; it concluded on "The Church: Bridging Space and Time."

A third series of 11 sermons was exclusively Christological, dealing with the life of Jesus. Its title (appropriate for the United *Kingdom*) was, JESUS, MONARCH OF MEN. The opening sermon was on the Divine Humanity. The continuation included studies of Jesus as: Boy and Apprentice, Jesus Baptized, Jesus Tempted, Jesus the Teacher, Jesus the Evangelist, the Social Thinker, the Healer, Man of Prayer, Worker of Wonders, Jesus Transfigured, and, finally, Jesus Enthroned in the Ascension.

I also preached briefer series of sermons such as 4 on 'Christ and Human Need', 3 on "The Divinity of our Lord", and 3 on "Christianity." The congregation attended them in good numbers, listened attentively, and thanked me generously for them. They kept me studying hard in the New Testament, in theological books, and in literary sources for illustrative materials. But above all the different series minimized the perennial dangers of subjectivity and idiosyncracy in the interpretation of Scripture.

The series referred to were kept chiefly for the morning congregation of the faithful members of the Church. For the evening congregations that included many strangers I used more controversial sermons. For example, the most controversial series of all was entitled, "The Challenge of the Sects" in which I analyzed the departures from historical and ecumenical Christian doctrines found in several modern sects, such as Christian Science, British Israel, the Mormons, Jehovah's Witnesses, Seventh Day Adventism, Moral Rearmament (formerly the Oxford Group), and Pentecostalism. It was my hope to make dialogue with these movements and to present their tenets as fairly as possible. What made the occasion unusually lively was the loud responses of the critics of the sermon in the congregation, defending those sects as members of them, and challenging me with their interruptions of my address, and causing much excitement because they would not wait to make their points in the after-meeting in the church hall.

Ultimately, about ten years later, these addresses appeared in the form of a book, published by the Student Christian Movement Press of London and the Abingdom Press of New York and Nashville under the title of *Christian Deviations: The Challenge of the Sects*. It was the most successful book I have ever written, selling over 150,000 copies in Britain and North America. It went into twelve impressions or revised editions and was translated into French, German, and Chinese.

If it was a major problem to find significant and relevant sermon topics, it was an even greater hardship for me to find suitable children's sermons. One was required every Sunday morning to hold the attention of the youngsters before they left for Children's Church, which was a half hour of the equivalent of Sunday School. We were one of the very earliest churches to introduce Children's Church. The point of this experiment was to enable the children to worship with their parents for the first half of the hour and then to receive in separate groups graduated instruction appropriate to their ages in classrooms. I was unusually fortunate in having two gifted ladies in the congregation to carry out this experiment. One had written magisterially about the new concept for the Religious Education Press and her name was Margaret Ferguson, and the other was, Nellie Lay, the mother of three boys, who was the superintendent of Children's Church. But this innovation made the children's sermon even more important than it had been previously, not to mention the Youth Service which was to be held on every fourth Sunday morning.

What, you may well ask, was so formidable about being required to prepare so many children's sermons? One was the tendency of the majority of the children's sermons that I had heard to be excessively and sloppily sentimental —to be examples of preaching down to the children rather than exercising their minds and stimulating their imaginations. Another difficulty was that of finding stories or illustrations that were not trivial and that correlated genuine Christian doctrine or devotion with authenticity, without which Christianity would become unbelievable. My search-

es for suitable stories or credible incidents or anecdotes
were varied and protracted.

In fact, the greatest relief I experienced in leaving
the pastoral ministry for the professoriate was that I had no
longer to prepare or deliver children's addresses!
The difficulty may be indicated by providing a single example of what I considered to be a good and truthful
story, which I used to illustrate the central importance of
the Scriptures. The text I wished to illustrate was I Corin-
thians 14:33, which reads: "God . . . the author." Since the
story was short and simple I will quote it in full:

> A little girl wanted to buy her father a Christmas present,
> so she saved up a lot of her pocket money. She also
> watched him very carefully to see what he liked. He was a
> learned man who taught in the university and he used to
> read a lot of books in his study. She noticed that sometimes
> when he was reading a book a little smile played about his
> mouth. Then she was really happy for she knew it would
> make him joyful if she got him a book.
> So she visited a bookshop and saw hundreds of books,
> some little and fat, some long and thin, some with pictures
> and some without. There were so many to choose from that
> she didn't know which to pick. Then, without knowing it,
> her Sunday School teacher helped her. Her teacher said:
> "The Bible's easily the best book in the world." So after
> school on Monday she rushed to the bookshop and bought
> a Bible.
> Then she crept into Daddy's study and wrote a message in-
> side the front page. Before writing it, she looked at some of
> Daddy's books to see what other people had put inside
> them. Her father was delighted with the present, but you
> can guess his surprise when he read the message which
> was just the words: "With the author's compliments."
> Wouldn't it be a good idea if we all wrote that inside our
> Bibles for in a special way He is the author of the Bible.
> The men who wrote this collection of stories and histories
> and letters had all learned first from God. And the messag-

es come with God's good wishes—"the Author's compli-
ments."

The gravest problem of all during the years 1942 to
1945 was the impact created by the German *Blitzkrieg* on
London and its satellite towns. This was particularly concentrated in our neighborhood because we were immediately adjacent to Croydon airport, a prime target for the planes
with fire bombs that flew across the English Channel. In
these days it was essential to darken windows to prevent
light getting through in what was known as the "blackout".
Air raid wardens patrolled the streets to check the com-
pleteness of the night's darkness. Street lamps as well as automobile lamps were hooded. Many children in the London
area were evacuated to other parts of England, Scotland and
Wales. On December 29,1940 the second Great Fire of
London took place and over 700 acres of London, a third of
the area, was destroyed by fire bombs that night. Southampton and Coventry had similar experiences. In central
London the only outstanding symbol of the divine was the
great Dome of St. Paul's Cathedral, a veritable beacon of
hope.

The fire bombs were bad enough, but the later V-1
buzz bombs were wearing down the resources of the citizens with their day and night incessant attacks. The only individuals who were really invulnerable were those who
took mattresses or their substitutes to the London Under-
ground stations at night, so vividly depicted in the drawings
of Henry Moore.

The V-1s, pilotless, looked like crossbows, and flew
like planes, although less rapidly. Their glow, given off by
their vapor trails, made them visible. Their noise caused
them to be named "buzz bombs" and their impact was all
the more fearful as they were unexpected. The British public had not been warned about their possible arrival. Although they could be seen, one never knew where they
might fall, because their flight might end forward or do a
sudden right or left turn. Imagine, then, what it was like to

sleep in the dampish basement of a totally blacked-out house and to hear the insistent buzzing, bugging sound above and not to know if the bomb would hit you or your neighbor's roof! The howling of sirens like dervishes destroyed sleep, and often only just anticipated by seconds the rocking explosions of the V-2s. In the days one reacted to the sirens by hiding beneath a table or desk. At night one either remained outdoors—in a flimsy Anderson shelter or indoors in the basement. It was enough simply to survive.

The more powerful V-2 rockets that followed the V-1s in the fifth year of the war created greater damages to houses and schools. They came at greater speed and could not be heard until they exploded. So their psychological effect was less disturbing. The town of Wallington received well over a hundred V-1 bombs. One V-1 bomb landed in the playground of the High School during a break from lessons and killed several young hopefuls. The only escape my wife and I were able to make was for a week one year when we led a group of young folk from the church youth-hostelling in the Lake District of North West England. Never did mountains seem easier to climb, nor lakes more attractive to swim in, and the actual loads on our backs were much lighter than the weight of woe in the blitz.

My deacons and I had devised two projects to take the minds of our congregation off the German air attacks. One was to hold study-groups at the houses of various members in adjacent streets. These proved to be a Godsend, because people could cheer each other up and by studying forget about the blitz. In this way we were able to continue effective Christian education among the adults. One year, as previously mentioned, Christian worship was our topic; the next year, the theme was Christian social ethics and the textbook Archbishop William Temple's *Christianity and Social Order*.

Our other experimental project was even more enterprising. We needed to think seriously and hopefully about the rebuilding of Europe after the war to enable us to get through the war years. We knew that many important leaders of European countries had sought refuge in England during the conquests of Hitler and Mussolini, and that these democrats might delight to lecture English folk on the future of their native lands. Thus it was that the Wallington Town Hall was filled with citizens once every month to hear, for example, Dr. Masaryk of Czechoslovakia, speak movingly about his hopes for his own country in the postwar years. Thus we heard leaders of France, Holland, Norway and Belgium, and other lands address us and I was privileged to be the undeserving chairman at these meetings that filled the Town Hall.

For a long time I had wished to undertake a more patriotic expression of the ministry, such as that of an army chaplain, but there were few such opportunities for Congregational ministers of my relatively young age. However, in September of 1945 I was given leave of absence from my church to serve as Director of Education of the British Young Men's Christian Association serving with the British Army of the Rhine. Our headquarters was at Badsalzuflen, near Bielefeld. To most servicemen the Y.M.C.A. was a place where they could get tea or coffee or cakes at the end of the day. My task as Director of Education was to provide educational and religious resources. I helped the Y.M.C.A. local secretaries in their various Army posts in Germany, Belgium and France after VE Day (Victory in Europe Day) to make preparation for Sunday evening worship in their centers by giving printed Orders of Worship which in their choice of hymns, Scripture lessons, and prayers provided an introduction to the Christian life. All theological terms were explained and an attempt was made to express ourselves in common but not vulgar language with relevance to their situation. I always included responses in the prayers so that they were human dialogs with God, not merely the voices of the leader. I must have prepared thirty or forty of such forms of Christian worship, but, of course, I have no idea as to how well or ill they were received.

My other task—a difficult but really worthwhile one—was to try to prepare the servicemen for employment upon their reinsertion into "civvy street." This meant that I had to interview German citizens who had the necessary skills and were willing to use them to teach British soldiers. Thus a German plumber was matched with a potential plumber, musician with musician, artist with artist, teacher with teacher. This was significant peacemaking after the trials of war. Thus when I returned to England I felt I had not only done my bit for Britain, but also a little for Germany.

Two personal memories of these days light up the past for me. One was the opportunity to hear the third really great man in my life, namely the former U-boat commander, Wilhelm Niemöller, pastor of the Berlin suburb of Dahlem, who had suffered years in prison by daring to condemn Fuehrer Hitler. I shall never forget his determined look and recall his extraordinary courage. The other two great men I had heard earlier were Archbishop William Temple and Dr. Albert Schweitzer.

The other memory was of an exceedingly simple meal spent the Sunday after Christmas in a German and Christian home in Bielefeld. We sat down to a lunch of a single course of soup in which there was floating a lump of something between suet and bread about the size of a golf-ball. Before the meal began we all joined hands round the table for the grace—a British soldier, a Scots lady in her middle sixties, myself, two German ladies, and a boy of five (a little fellow named Pretzel). The mother, the aunt, and the children present sang to us in German "Welcome in the name of Christ." As we linked hands we knew another Christian bridge had been built for the future. Easy enough, you might respond. Was it easy for our hostess to invite us? Her husband, a chaplain, was ill in a French prisoner of war camp; and her two brothers, also chaplains, had been killed on the Russian front. It is the pierced, wounded shining and forgiving hands of Christ that form the Bridge over the waters of suspicion.

My greatest joy on my return to Wallington church was to be present at the birth of my daughter, Christine, a warm and tender child who now has a deep Christian faith. One of the ways her mother, Brenda, used to help me was at the church door when the members of the congregation were leaving, by reminding me of the names of the persons whose hands I was about to shake. I thought my memory was good, but hers was better; I could recall historical dates but she remembered living persons. Although she had passed the University entrance examination, Brenda elected to go to Westhill Training College in Birmingham where she gained a Froebel diploma, qualifying her to teach young children at which she was very capable, as also at music, whether piano or recorder. This training was invaluable for the upbringing of our children, who eventually were three. The thought of leaving her country for the first time with a small infant for a very remote land must have been extremely disquieting for her, but she bravely accepted her new responsibility. Our next destination was South Africa.

3

LIFE IN SOUTH AFRICA: 1947-1953

On a bitterly cold December day in 1947 Brenda, my wife, Christine our daughter not yet a year old, and I left Southampton on The Winchester Castle, a Union-Castle liner. My cartons of books, snow drenched, reached me over three months later, with battered covers and dissolving interiors—a serious disadvantage for a professor teaching a new discipline in a university college that had a few volumes of theology or church history on its shelves, and I had immediately to plan new courses with required readings.

We were bound for the Union of South Africa, then in European high esteem because its leader was General Smuts, a member of the British Commonwealth's Imperial Council, and a distinguished philosopher, whose Deputy Prime Minister was Jan Hofmeyr, a notably bright and compassionate Christian. Our sea journey would take us three weeks in time and over 6,000 miles in space. The women with children were placed in the cabins of officers on the upper deck, while the men were jammed like sardines in standees three deep in the bowels of the ship. It was not a joy ride although we were routed through the Mediterranean and via the Suez Canal. We stopped briefly at Cairo, then Aden, where the temperature was in the high nineties at eleven o'clock at night, and where they had not had any rain for six years—so we were told. On the way down the East Coast of Africa we stopped at Mombasa, Kenya's attractive port, at Lourenco Marques the main port of Mozambique, and, finally, we disembarked at Durban,

where we were welcomed by Stanley Craven, formerly a
member of the church in Thornton, Yorkshire, with whose
friends we broke our journey. After three weeks in the total
company of strangers it was a joy to renew friendship.
After a day or two we continued our journey by
train via Port Elizabeth to Grahamstown, arriving on January
23, 1947. Grahamstown was to be our home for the ensuing
seven years. This small but attractive city had been
founded in 1820 by English settlers. It was 80 miles from a
large city, Port Elizabeth, and 30 miles from a small seaside
village, Port Alfred. Grahamstown was dominated by a
lengthy main street with its neo-Gothlc Anglican cathedral,
its large Settlers' Memorial Methodist Church, and it contained
contrasts that were striking.
At its upper end (both socially and geographically)
were the impressive buildings of the University College,
with their white stucco walls and red-tiled roofs, entered by
the Drosdy Arch, a historical military erection, and at the
lower end, by the rather rundown houses of the Cape Coloreds,
and the miserable huts of the Africans. The Center of
the street contained food, fashion and bookshops, but the
contrast between rich and poor, clearly ethnic in character,
was shocking.
After renting a home for about a year, we bought a
modest ranch house on the hillside, with a small front lawn,
an orchard that seemed exotic to us with its orange and
lemon trees, and its magnificent purple jacarandas, not forgetting
its eighty rose bushes. I remember two small incidents
vividly in that garden. One was when I undeservedly
became a hero to my family, when I killed a boomslang, a
tree snake, which seemed to menace our daughter Christine.
The other, amusingly, was seeing the Christmas turkey
being carried off in the mouth of our own cunning dog.
Grahamstown was to be our home for seven eventful years,
during which our first son, Hugh Marlais, was born in
1948.
What were we doing in South Africa anyway? The
story begins in the late spring of 1946. when Principal
Micklem of Mansfield College, Oxford, sent a letter to me

in Germany announcing that Rhodes University College in Grahamstown desired to appoint a Professor of Divinity to create a new department of Divinity. I applied and two distinguished British professors were kind enough to write me glowing recommendations. One was John Baillie, Professor of Divinity at Edinburgh University, who has previously taught at Union Theological Seminary in New York City, and the other was F. L. Cross, Lady Margaret Professor of Divinity in the University of Oxford.

On the strength of these recommendations, I was invited by the secretary of the interviewing committee, Canon Adam Fox of Westminster Abbey, to be present at South Africa House in Trafalgar Square, London. Since the chair was funded by the Anglican, Methodist, Presbyterian and Congregational Churches in South Africa, each church was entitled to a representative on the committee. Only that of the Congregationalists failed to appear!

My views were sought on the most important branches of divinity, such as theology (on its doctrinal side and on its defenses against criticism known as "apologetics"), on the important developments of Church History, and on Biblical Studies. They also tested the genuineness of my enthusiasm for ecumenism, namely the desirability of the reunion of all Christian denominations. I had anticipated these types of questions, and as I left the interview, I gave them a typed copy of the kinds of courses I would attempt to establish, if I were to be appointed.

While any appointment would require the ratification of the Rhodes University College Senate, it was fortunate that its Master, Dr. J. Smeath Thomas, was present at the interviewing committee and happened to be an elder of the Grahamstown Presbyterian Church. In the meantime, I was seriously considering an appointment to teach Church History in a central Chinese University, which presented linguistic and potentially political difficulties in the unsettled state of that vast country. Fortunately, I had only to wait two or three weeks before news of my South African appointment arrived, and I accepted immediately.

I retain a copy of the conditions of appointment.

The salary was 750 pounds sterling per annum, with a married cost of living allowance of 80 pounds, double my salary as a minister. The applicant had to make himself familiar with Afrikaans within three years. Some theological courses had to be provided for the B. A. degree, a condition unknown in Scotland or in the Dutch Reformed Seminaries of South Africa, where all divinity degrees were postgraduate. The head of the new department of Divinity could be expected to organize the instruction in the department and would have the assistance of two or possibly three part-time lecturers, who might be resident wardens of hostels under the control of the cooperating Churches. No indication was given at this stage that the approval for all the courses would be required to be given by the federal University of South Africa, of which Rhodes University College was a constituent member. That was a difficulty that would have to be faced soon after my arrival.

A greatly admired colleague, Leslie Hewson, accompanied me to the decisive meetings of the University of South Africa held on February 13th and following days in Durban. As a Classics graduate of the University of the Witwatersrand in Johannesburg, and afterwards a first class honors B. A. in theology of the University of Cambridge, who was South African born and raised and was also fluent in Afrikaans, his presence was invaluable. Fortunately, as a prop to my memory of these days, he wrote an article to the most popular South African weekly magazine, the *Outspan*, entitled "A New Era in Theological Training". Many years later, his fuller account of the early years came in a *festschrift* presented to me on my retirement in 1984 from Princeton University.

Was what we were attempting to establish indeed "A New Era in Theological Training"? Already there were three Afrikaans medium Universities or University Colleges in South Africa, with theological seminaries in Stellenbosch, Pretoria and Potchefstroom, but there was no English-medium University or University college to train English-medium South African ministers to-be. So our work was *new* in that respect.

It was also novel in that each of the Afrikaans medium institutions were centers for the theological training of one or another divisions of the family of Dutch Reformed Churches, whereas we were inter-denominational and committedly ecumenical. As for our difficulties, they were compounded by the fact that our opposite number as a constituent college in the federal University of South Africa was named the Potchefstroom University College for Christian Higher Education. It was theologically the most traditional and the most conservative college and therefore suspicious of our approach, especially as their theological students were all post-graduate and began the Bachelor Degree only after completing the Bachelor of Arts degree.

Our proposals must have seemed at first both excessively liberal in character (although both I and my colleagues were, in fact, neo-orthodox, but certainly not fundamentalists) as well as being apparently superficial. And here I cannot refrain from citing Canon B. H. Streeter's witty definition of a fundamentalist as one who finds fun in damning the mental. In fact, the fundamentalist's concern for basic Biblical doctrine is a determination to take the Bible with the utmost seriousness. For him it is the infallible Word of God, and he refuses to dilute it to make it acceptable.

I trust that I may be excused for quoting Leslie Hewson's impressions of the task and of the one who was chiefly responsible. Speaking of myself, he wrote in *The Livingstonian* thirteen years after the events the following:

> He had the responsibility of planning the academic side of theological training, and he was admirably suited to his task. He was a brilliant scholar [a friendly exaggeration] and was determined that the new scheme should be of academic repute.
>
> He was a bonny fighter, and there was much prejudice to be overcome and many practical difficulties to be surmounted. He was also an ardent ecumenist, an essential qualification in a scheme which was a bold venture of faith in Christian cooperation. He had moreover a charm and a

gift for friendship, which I believe was never more effec-
tively realized than in the historic meetings of the Senate
of the University of South Africa at Durban in 1947 . . . I
was permitted to accompany Dr. Davies to act as a liaison
with the members of the Divinity department of Potchefstroom University College. This was the only other constituent college engaged in theological studies, and Dr.
Davies had been warned by well-meaning, but misguided folk that
he, a British theologian, would be opposed and thwarted in
his plans by the men of Potchefstroom to whom his nationality and his theology would be anathema.

Shades of the effects of the Anglo-Boer war in the
last decade of the nineteenth century were still lurking
around !

The decisive series of meetings were held on April
10 and 11, 1947 at Howard College of the University College of Natal. Immediately after lunch, I had a long talk
with professor du Toit of Potchefstroom and his numerous
questions ended with the challenge: "What do you think of
the Higher Criticism". Soon afterwards, a full divinity committee met, strengthened by the presence of the principal of
Potchefstroom, Dr. Postma, their professor of philosophy,
Dr. Stoker and professors Jooste and du Toit. We two and a
silent member from Grahamstown were outnumbered. In
discussing our proposal, I provided the background, indi-
cating that the Methodist Church, with the largest number
of intending students, proposed that matriculants and those
without a certificate of University entrance, would be allowed to spend only three years at Rhodes. Hence a B. A.
with theological options was essential for the graduands
and a diploma for their non-matriculants, who in fact, were
few. Our other denominations preferred a stronger curriculum in which a B. A. was followed by a B.D. post-graduate
degree. The Potchefstroom Principal declared that the necessary basis for any professional degree must be a general
degree, which he stated had been reaffirmed that very afternoon in the Senate.

I argued that a B. A. with theological options would be invaluable also for teachers in secondary schools and for any Christian student who wished to strengthen his or her faith, and I pointed out that there was an analogy for this already in the British Universities. This won general interest, but it was when the three year major of Biblical Studies was proposed, and the single course in Ecclesiastical History as an alternative to History II, that the tide began to turn.

But when the two year major in Theology was proposed, the tide turned against us again. They demanded to know how theology could possibly be a major subject in an *Arts* degree. They insisted that this would require a lowering of the standards of Theology. After the meeting, du Toit asked Hewson if the Methodist Church would agree to a longer period of training. But Hewson said that he had no authority to agree to that.

When we returned the next morning, du Toit and Jooste proposed a new solution. Why not call the new courses part of a diploma of Theology, not a degree? This I rejected immediately because a diploma is inferior to a degree. Finally, however, when I outlined the actual courses and their proposed contents, the last vestiges of opposition finally disappeared. In Hewson's words: "It was an unexpected triumph, for at two stages, last night and today, it seemed we had no hope."

One further obstacle in this race seemed formidable in anticipation—that was to get the entire faculty of Arts, which was to convene that very afternoon, to sanction our proposal. The members might well regard Divinity as a mere intruder among the Humanities. In fact, Durrant, the professor of English at Natal University College, insisted that knowledge of the Bible should be presupposed in English Studies. Professor Hartmann of Rhodes said the same was true for music. Our final feeling of relief was: "All's well that ends well."

It seemed so important to me that the cooperating Churches should be aware of the nature of the disciplines of Theology at this time (and it may be advantageous for non-theological readers today) that I wrote two articles for *The*

Presbyterian Leader, showing their relevance and their contents, which I now summarize.

The four Departments of Divinity, Old Testament, New Testament, Systematic Theology, and Church History, spring from the very nature of our Christian Faith. We are Christians because of the Revelation of the acts of God, the Creator and Sustainer, culminating in the Incarnation, the Cross and the Resurrection and Ascension of Jesus Christ the Messiah and the gift of the Holy Spirit, to which the prophets and the apostles are the chief witnesses. Their witness was committed to sacred writings and communicated by the Church as the community and body of Christ. Clearly, the first interest of the future minister of God's Word, contained in the Old and New Testament is to understand it, preferably in the original languages of Hebrew and Hellenistic Greek. Systematic Theology is the necessary explication and defense of the Biblical faith, and Church History is studied both as an encouragement and a warning, for it is both the continuation of "The Acts of the Apostles" and the acts of Judas Iscariot!

In the sub-disciplines, important new emphases have been reached. For the sake of brevity, it can be said that early in this century in Biblical Studies, there were two schools of thought, which have since been labeled fundamentalists and modernists. The former was so styled because they clung to the infallibility of the written Word. The latter, called modernists, welcomed the historical approach to the Bible. The merit of the first group was their adherence to orthodoxy that of the second school was that it eagerly embraced historical, critical and archeological aids to the understanding of the Bible. Its weakness was, that in its insistence upon the human and fallible recipients of Divine Revelation, the Bible tended to become a literary puzzle and the Gospel diluted into the Fatherhood of God and the Brotherhood of Humankind. (This despite the fact that the New Testament knows of no automatic religious brotherhood or sisterhood, but only one by adoption by Jesus Christ.)

It soon became clear that neither option would do,

since neither a "paper-pope" nor a textbook of human opinion about God would help. Theologians cried, "A plague on both your houses". Thus under the influence of Karl Barth and Emil Brunner (though P. T. Forsyth had anticipated both), the post-critical approach to the Bible was developed in which the standard was the orthodoxy of the Apostles and the Niceno-Constantinopolitan creeds as faithful summaries of the central Biblical doctrines, or, in a word, neo-orthodoxy. Its British exponents were T. W. Manson, a Presbyterian, C. H. Dodd and H. Cunliffe-Jones, Congregationalists, Vincent Taylor and Norman Snaith, Methodists, H. H. Rowley and H. Wheeler Robinson, Baptists and Sir Edwyn Hoskyns and Noel Davey, Anglicans. In the U.S.A. its exponents were Reinhold Niebuhr and his brother H. Richard Niebuhr who both belonged to the United Church of Christ. This approach used the aids of scholarship to ask the historical questions: what did God say, for example to Moses? Then it went on to ask: What is God's Word to us through Moses and Jesus Christ today?

Systematic Theology is customarily divided into two sections or studies. The one is Christian Dogmatics, which expounds the historic doctrines of Christian faith: God as Creator of the world, and his providence; the doctrines of the person and work of Jesus Christ; the doctrines of the Holy Spirit as illuminator, inspirer, sanctifier, and the bond of unity; and eschatology: the doctrines of the last Things: Death, Judgment, Heaven and Hell. But the second branch is known as Apologetics- the defense of Christianity against its critics who have challenged it as philosophers, scientists, psychologists, or sociologists, not to mention the claims of other religions. Because the Christian Faith aims at changing individuals and systems, a study of Christian Ethics was essential in this country of complex ethnic constitution .

Ecclesiastical History, once a dry catalogue of orthodox saints and horrific heretics has found a new importance in the twentieth century. Three new emphases have been stressed in the more recent writing of Church History under the influence and the example of one of the greatest

contemporary theological historians, Professor Kenneth Latourette of Yale University Divinity School. First, he taught
the divided Churches to look beyond their own frontiers to
recount the gains and losses of world Christianity. Sectari-
an ecclesiastical history, with its monotonous beating of the
denominational drum has been outmoded by the Ecumenical Movement. The second emphasis in modern Church
History is stressing important parallels for our instruction
between "Then and Now," such as the emperor-worship of
the first and second centuries A.D. and the totalitarian deifi-
cation of political leaders in Germany and Italy and Japan
in the twentieth century; also between Gnosticism of yes-
terday and Christian Science and Spiritualism today., The
third emphasis must be on the amazing missionary expansion of the Church in the past 175 years. Church historians
can no longer relegate "Foreign Missions" to an appen-
dix—the only truly foreign territory for the Church is
where the Gospel has not penetrated, or where it has been
repudiated. The Church is either missionary or it is a
corpse.

The rest of that year was full of excitement. First
the Senate of our own university college had to approve the
syllabi that we were presenting for our studies, and the
plans for establishing a theological hostel for the Congregationalists, Presbyterians and Methodists. In September and
October the supreme bodies of these Churches would be
meeting to ratify our plans, and it was my task to make the
successive presentations. The ministers, guiding the plans
for the Hostel, were chaired by a devout layman, Dr. Alex-
ander Kerr, who was the Head of the South African Native
College at Fort Hare in nearby Alice. They included our
two part-time lecturers: Leslie Hewson, a Methodist, was to
be the first Warden of the future Livingtone House, and our
lecturer in Apologetics, the Revd. John McDowall, who
had taken an Honours degree in zoology at Glasgow University, had lectured in Zoology at Fort Hare, and was minister of the Presbyterian Church in Grahamstown. After the
war, there was a great shortage of buildings but Rhodes
University received a priority for its new Divinity Hostel. It

was erected a year after our first meeting and included an admirably simple chapel. Leslie Hewson rightly insisted that: "There will be no attempt to ignore or minimise the different denominational traditions which we inherit. No tree can bear the proper fruit unless it is firmly rooted in one particular soil; and those who proudly claim that they are 'just Christians' usually merit the comment 'Yes, and only just!'"

It was understood that the University College at Fort Hare, some sixty miles to the north of Grahamstown, was under our aegis and that our syllabi in Divinity would also apply to their students. I deliberately stipulated that the students, both Africans and Cape Coloureds, should be expected to attain the same standards as the Caucasians did at Rhodes University College. This would, in my view, demonstrate their intellectual competence. I was glad to take this anti-racist stand. In fact, since the Africans used English only as their second language (setting aside their own native Bantu tongue), and their lectures and required readings were almost exclusively English, it might well have required greater competence on their part than that demanded for the "Europeans" The latter was the South African term for Caucasians, often pejoratively contrasted with the negative term for the Africans and Coloureds, namely "NonEuropeans". I shall deal with the racism of South Africa and the Afrikaans term "apartheid" (separateness) at greater length later.

In 1948 the Calendar of Rhodes University College gave the first published official record of the new Department. It read as follows:

DIVINITY
Professor Horton Davies
and Part-time Lecturer

Divinity courses may be taken for the B.A. degree, in combination with any non theological courses. Courses are also given in preparation for the post-graduate B.D. degree. There are two B.A. Divinity Majors: *Biblical Studies* (a

course lasting three years) and *Systematic Theology* (a
course lasting two years). In addition *Ecclesiastical History* may be taken as a minor course.

In a specially prepared "Divinity Prospectus" the
aims of the Department were expounded. It was emphasized that since the Chair had been financed by the contributions of the Anglican, Congregational, Methodist, and
Presbyterian Churches of South Africa, training for the
ministry of these Churches would be its primary, though
not exclusive purpose. It was stressed that the Department
was ecumenical in origin and in purpose, and that its staff
included ministers of the contributing Churches and its students belonged to these four Communions. In addition
however, students of the Baptist and Disciples of Christ denominations were also included. Then it added: "At the
same time the Department of Divinity is prepared to give
every possible co-operation in training candidates for the
Ministry accredited by any Christian denomination."

Then a novelty was advertised: "It will welcome in-
quiries from teachers intending to specialize in Religious
Instruction in Schools, and from intending Youth Leaders
who will work for the Churches or allied Christian Youth
organizations (such as the Y.M.C.A.) and Missionary candidates." It was possible to propose these additions because
of the cooperation offered by two friends on the faculty,
Professor Monica Wilson, Head of the Department of Bantu Studies, and Professor James Irving, Head of the-
Department of Sociology, both persons of high professional
competence and profound compassion .

Professor Hewson comments on that Prospectus
thirty years later:

> After more than thirty years, reflection upon that prospec-
> tus shows two things that merit comment. The first is that
> Rhodes University College in 1947 through its first Profes-
> sor of Divinity pioneered theological studies in English-
> medium universities in South Africa. Following approval
> by the University of South Africa of the Rhodes proposal

to introduce divinity subjects into an Arts degree, Religious Studies are now recognized and provided in every South African university. The second is that the final paragraph formulating the aims of the Department still stands substantially the same through the administrations of the four Heads of Deapartment and Deans of the Faculty of Divinity who have succeeded Dr. Davies at Rhodes. They still affirm, and aspire to practice the Lordship of Jesus Christ and the supreme relevance of the Christian Revelation to our contemporary situation; and they are still committed to work ecumenically, in obedience to the Dominical intercession, *ut omnes unum sint* (that all may be one).

I had an admirable opportunity locally to set forth my ecumenical intentions in an inaugural lecture given on June 9, 1948, which was entitled "Towards an Ecumenical Theology and a United Church."

I began this inaugural lecture by pointing out how appropriate the theme was, since in August of 1948 almost 150 different Communions of the Universal or Ecumenical Church would be meeting in Amsterdam to inaugurate the World Council of Churches. I confessed that I was not in the least perturbed to be an advocate of Ecumenism or even called an "Ecumaniac" since I believed that if "this is madness, there is method in it," and recalled that the greatest of the apostles was content to be thought "a fool for Christ's sake."

Next I proceeded to explore six aspects of Ecumenism: first, its *desirability;* second, its potential *dangers;* third, some *designs* for unity; fourth, *divisive* factors; fifth, *demonstrations* of unity achieved; and last, the need for a *Dedication* to Ecumenism.

The theological basis was strongly stressed based on Christ's High Priestly Prayer as translated by Moffatt: "Nor do I pray for them alone, but for all who believe in me by their spoken word; may they all be one." and I added St. Paul's plea to the Church in Corinth: " Brothers, for the sake of our Lord Jesus Christ I beg of you drop these party cries. . . Has Christ been parcelled out?" I further argued that partial theological emphases had been safeguarded by individual denominations or sects throughout history as if these were all the truth to the confusion of many. Such cliques destroyed the peace and the spread of the worldwide Church.

The dangers I saw in Ecumenism were three. First, there is the possibility of devising a scheme of reunion on the lowest level of agreement amongst the Churches; such syncretism is what G. K. Chesterton called "religion going to pot." Another danger is the possibility that Ecumenism might compromise truth by convenient formulae cloaking basic disagreements. The third criticism is that uniformity of Churchmanship could diminish if not destroy the life of the Spirit of the Churches.

As I look back on the formative years of the Department of Divinity, it seems excessively ambitious to have tried to establish it with myself as the single full-time member for the first eighteen months, with the help of four part-time lecturers. Even for the subsequent five and a half years of my stay at Rhodes, we were only two full-time faculty members, with the addition of William Cosser, a graduate in Arts and Divinity at Glasgow University, who had done futher studies at the University of Strasbourg and was endowed with a pawky sense of humor. The part-timers were, however, men of great quality and unquenchable enthusiasm. They included F.C. Synge, the Warden of the St. Paul's (Church of the Province) Anglican Theological College, and an able theologian, the Revd. John McDowall, the Revd. Charles Stephenson, chaplain at Kingswood School in Grahamstown, who was invaluable for his instruction in the diploma of theology for the intending teachers of religious instruction. Leslie Hewson proved an admirable colleague. Shortly after my leaving Rhodes, with the arrival of new funding, he was rightly promoted to the position of full-time professor of New Testament. He represented continuity, ecumenism, and enthusiasm in the Divinity Department until his retirement. These men were remarkable pioneers to whom Rhodes University owes a great deal.

I can remember how surprised and amused the distinguished faculty of Union Theological Seminary in New York City were (including Paul Tillich and Reinhold Niebuhr) when I spoke to them about the beginnings of theology at Rhodes. I told them that we had such a minuscule divinity library and a small annual grant for new books that, in desperation, I put an advertisement in *The Christian Recorder* asking ministers who were willing to part with any theological books in good condition to despatch them to us! This was the nucleus of our Divinity library. Later, of course, our holdings became more substantial.

Life was exciting but also exhausting in my early years in South Africa, with entire sets of new lectures to prepare, articles to write that, while maintaining professional integrity, would help to put our Department of Divinity on the map or enable me to combat racism. Somehow I also managed to make time to produce three books, one of which, happily, was co-authored. I also wrote my "Ministers for Tomorrow" article which the renowned *Hibbert Journal* of London published in April 1950 (Vol. XLVIII). In it I suggested that future ministers would need to be teachers rather than converters, but also missionaries in an increasingly materialistic world, experimenters, and profoundly ecumenical. And I stressed that the spirit of the ministers must be a compassion that deflates all conformity, making them class and color-blind.

In Church History, it seemed important to me to make the South African theological students proud of their past leaders, especially if they were liberal in race relations. For this reason I wrote a series of brief biographies of important Christians, many of them missionaries of the Dutch or English Churches at work in South Africa. These appeared in the widely read weekly, *The Outspan,* and were illustrated by our friend, Grace Lloyd-Evans who had gained her diploma at the Royal College of Art in London. They formed the basis of my book, *Great South African Christians.* They were chosen to represent variety of nationality, differences of Christian allegiance, and diversities of Christian service. Some were famous, and all deserved

to be. Their names were: George Schmidt, John Philip,
Robert Moffatt, William Shaw, Daniel Lindley, Robert
Gray, Eugene Casalis, David Livingstone, Francis Pfanner,
Andrew Murray, Khama Boikano, Francois Coillard, Jan
Lion Cachet, Stefanus Hofmeyr, Ernest Creux and Paul
Berthoud, Mother Cecile and John White. The first was
born in 1709 and the last in 1866. This book was published
by the Cape Town branch of the Oxford University Press in
1951.

A second book was written in collaboration with the
Revd. Dr. R. H. W. Shepherd, Principal of the famous
Lovedale Missionary Institution, who was honored later as
Moderator of the Church of Scotland. This book was an anthology and its title was *South African Missions 1800-1950*.
It appeared, a year after I had left South Africa, in 1954 and
was published by Thomas Nelson and Sons of London and
Edinburgh. The volume aimed to show the settings, the variety of missionary service, and the distinction of missionaries. Its chapter headings will give some indication of the
flavor of the book. The first eight chapters bore the following titles: The peoples of South Africa; Customs; Pre-
Christian Ideas; Witch-finders; Climate, Flora and Fauna;
Environment, Travelling; and Chiefs. The last eight chapters were entitled: Caesar's Attitude; Critics; Missionaries;
Famous Mission Stations; Techniques, Problems; Converts
and their Ways; and The Benefits of Missions.

Since we were teaching only South African students
and our degrees were all from European universities, Bill
Cosser, our senior Lecturer, and I thought we might appear
less foreign if we prepared dissertations for the Doctor of
Divinity degree of the University of South Africa, which
we eventually gained. I had, about this time, been approached by Gilbert Murray, the famous Oxford University
classical scholar, on the recommendation of Principal Nathaniel Micklem, to write a book on the contribution of the
Baptists, Congregationalists, Methodists, Presbyterians, and
Quakers to the life of England in the well-known series
"The Home University Library." So I wrote this history and
killed two birds with this stone, which was both a disserta-

tion and a book: *The English Free Churches*. It was published by Oxford University Press in 1952. A second edition appeared in England in 1963, and a third American edition in 1985.

My conclusion, much abbreviated, will indicate the convictions that the book expressed. I felt that the Free Churches were custodians of four important principles: first, the Church is a "gathered" community, their Christians are not born so but are made by the Divine initiative and the human surrender of faith. Next, their forms of church polity conserve "the Crown rights of Christ as Redeemer", and His exclusive right to rule in the churches, unfettered by the dictates of hierarchy or the favor of Caesar. Thirdly, the Free Churches are democratic and witness to "the priesthood of all believers". Lastly, their recognition of the primacy of the Gospel over the Church, of revelation over its institutional expressions, has given them an elasticity and flexibility rarely evident in Catholic ecclesial structures." "But", I concluded, "like other Communions they pray for the fulfillment of our Lord's High-priestly prayer *ut omnes unum sint*, believing they have treasures to receive as well as to give, forgiveness to beg and to grant, in the One Holy Catholic and Apostolic Church *Visible* that is to be."

Life in South Africa was not all work; it included holidays. Often we visited that loveliest of African cities, Cape Town, dominated by its majestic Table Mountain on which a flat cloud often rested like a table-cloth, and at its feet were many parks, satellite suburbs, and beaches.

Having lived in the Eastern part of the Cape Province where history was only just a little over a hundred years old, it was a delight to see the ancient buildings of Cape Town which was first visited by the Dutch sailor Van Riebeck in the mid-seventeenth century. Occasionally I was invited, while the minister of a leading Cape Town Church was on summer vacation, to undertake the Sunday services in return for occupying the manse free of charge. This was the case at the Gardens Presbyterian Church where the minister was the Revd. Dr. P. B. Hawkridge.

I also preached at Methodist and Congregational Churches as far from Grahamstown as Durban or Johannesburg, or even Salisbury, in what was in those days known as Southern Rhodesia. Friends who often shared these vacations and were near neighbors were Professor James Irving and his vivacious wife, Dolly, and their lively daughter Janet. On the face of it the friendship seemed curious by virtue of the fact that Irving was a Marxist and I a Christian, but we shared negatively a loathing for racism in every form and positively a deep compassion. We were both attracted by the ethnic variety of South Africa.

Few who live outside South Africa are aware of its ethnic complexity and variety, or the proportionate size of each major ethnic group in the totality. At a rough estimate, there are a total of about 30 million South Africans, of whom 21 millions are Blacks, 5 millions are Whites, 3 millions are Coloreds, and 1 million are Asians. The Blacks came originally from Central Africa, and the largest tribal elements among them are the Zulus and the Xhosas, with smaller groups represented by the Northern and Southern Sothos, the Tswanas, the Shangaan-Tsongas, and the Swazis. Most of the Whites are descended from Dutch settlers who came first in the seventeenth and later centuries, and secondly from the British who arrived in strength at the start of the nineteenth century, with an addition of French and German settlers. The Coloreds included about 200,000 of Cape Malays inhabiting the Cape peninsula.

The first Asians arrived about 1860 to work on Natal's sugar-cane fields and over 85% of the Indians of South Africa live in Natal. The other Asians, in smaller groups, are Pakistanis, Sri Lankans, and Chinese. It is significant that there is an impressive Jewish population of about an eighth of a million persons the majority of whom live in Johannesburg. Many of them are proponents of social justice. Obviously, exciting as this variety of colors and cultures is, the fight for social and ethnic justice is bound to be long and bitter and the white minority has been reluctant to give up its privileges, political and economic. In my time there, with the advent of Dr. Malan and the increased Nationalist party of the Afrikaaners, the light for racial progress was only what the striking of a single match could produce!

Two visits that I made in Southern Africa left a deep impression. The first was a visit to South Africa's largest Leper Hospital which was located at Westport, a few miles out of Pretoria. Here there were eleven hundred lepers of all races, although Africans greatly predominated. My guide was Miss Creux of the Swiss Mission, and quite appropriately so, because Ernest Creux, the co-founder of the Swiss mission, was the first missionary to begin work amongst lepers in the Transvaal. As this able lady went on her rounds, I heard her addressing the women in Shangaan, Zulu, and Sesuto, all the while commenting to me in perfect English. Besides, she was brought up to speak French and German as her mother tongues. We saw many of these afflicted creatures, suffering from either the nodular or the neural type of leprosy. The former have misshapen faces, but few hid them at the compassionate missionary's approach. The latter have lost part of their limbs (fingers or toes) or entire limbs, or are partly paralysed or blind, but they gratefully held their stumps of hands together to receive the little gifts that Miss Ernst brought them as tokens of friendship.

This could have been a most depressing visit, but in fact it was immensely cheering. Why so? Because medical science now has the cure if the disease is diagnosed early enough. Sulphur drugs are the miracle-workers, and two of them each about the size of a large aspirin are taken daily. The old treatment consisted either of injections of a certain oil which was an emollient rather than a cure. Sometimes it was necessary for patients to take twenty one pills per day for several months. My informant told me that a cynical doctor on the staff at Westport used to say: "You can hear the patients rattle when they turn over in bed."

The old methods have gone, and no longer need the leper feel that he or she is a foul, nameless being, who must be shut out from human society, calling out "unclean" and ringing a bell to warn healthy citizens of his or her approach. Lepers are, of course, still isolated at Westport; but the women have their own rondavels (or little huts) which they kept spotlessly clean, and the men have their own houses which are untidier, as one might expect. The fitter men and women engage in all kinds of jobs in the colony and are able to earn money for comforts. There are playing fields and orchards and three superb chapels: Anglican, Roman Catholic and Free Church. The church built by the Swiss Mission and used by lepers of all the Free Churches is called "The Church of the Children of God." Its simple, white-washed brick walls are adorned by a splendid painting by Monsieur Robert, who has never seen South Africa, but who must have given immense pleasure to both lepers and visitors, for it depicts Jesus surrounded by lepers and is set in a riot of proteas, bougainvilleas, hisbisci and cannas, with shy buck peering from the bush. Christ in Africa amongst the lepers! So here are three allies: missionaries, doctors, and artists all working for the glory of God in the healing of the nations.

We also visited the Roman Catholic chapel where there were art treasures painted free of charge by the world-renowned Royal Academician, Sir Frank Brangwyn. On a previous visit to Westport I was told that the old Catholic priest had been a friend of Brangwyn many years before and had obtained from him a promise to paint fourteen Stations of the Cross for the chapel, and that the artist fulfilled his commission as his last large work of art, when worldly fame meant nothing and the golden citadels of eternity beckoned. So these poor lepers were enriched by looking at these representations of the suffering Savior, which an artist friend told me would have sold for about two thousand pounds sterling each. I do not regret that these treasures are not to be seen in the great Art Galleries of South Africa. I only regret that they do not attract more visitors to Westport to offer practical support for this splendid work of self-sacrifice.

My second memorable visit was to a remarkable mission-station in Southern Rhodesia, not many miles away from the town of Bulawayo, which commemorated an African's role at the Crucifixion, where he carried the Cross of

Christ. This was Simon of Cyrene. What made Cyrene mission-station unique was that it proclaimed the Christian Gospel almost exclusively through art. My attention was first drawn to it by a remarkable sign-board of enamelled white on which there was a single symbol, and, if I recall aright, it bore no name. But no name was necessary because the black cross tilted onto its side proclaimed the invisible cross-bearer of Cyrene. It was a mission-station supported by the Anglican Church of the Province of South Africa, and its head was Canon Edward Patterson, who made it a center for Christian art-lovers, but also more than that. He proved here that Africans are able artists. Anyone who thinks that African boys are only shabbily-dressed, down-at-heels, imitators of Caucasians should have come with me to a hut where four African boys were working at their benches. Two of them were cripples: the toes of one were literally growing out of his knee. But what beauty these ugly, crippled bodies created by compensation! These cripples were carving ivory statuettes of the Virgin or delicate deer in exquisite fashion. Another was painting a superb water-color tapestry of variegated foliage, with snakes, springboks, and multicolored birds, reminiscent of Persian art or of the dream world of the Douanier Rousseau.

If you had followed me to the chapel with its rounded apse you would have been enchanted by a whitewashed exterior to see in the blues, yellows, mauves and oranges of a Vincent Van Gogh the depiction of the Annunciation. But this multi-colored act of praise is a Mashona's, not a Dutchman's tribute to Christ. Then, finally, I would have taken you inside the chapel and shown you a carved Calvary which is Africa's own impression of the Crucifixion. A black Bantu Christ hangs from the rood, and it is a Bantu Madonna with a doek (or bandana) on her head who gazes on her suffering Son. Beehive huts, studding Calvary's hill, complete this masterpiece of African religious art. That it is a masterpiece is proven by the fact that an exact replica adorns the altar of the London Chapel of the Society for the Propagation of the Gospel. When I finally returned to Eng-

land in 1953, it was my privilege to share much of the time
on our ship, talking to Canon Patterson who had brought
with him as a gift for myself an African Cross with the Madonna and St. John looking up at the suffering Lord, with
rondavels in the background. Throughout my days in South
Africa, I was deeply troubled by the widespread racism. It
came home to me in the African and Cape Colored Congregational Ministers I came to know as personal friends, because in Grahamstown I was the consulent or adviser of
two of them. Their pay was wretchedly insufficient, and
their homes were virtually clean slums. In every way, they
were made to feel inferior to the whites. At the beaches,
there were signs saying bluntly: "Non-Europeans keep out."
They had to sit apart at the back of the buses. Their men
who worked hard for a pittance were forbidden to create labor unions for their economic self-defense. The women
served as children-minders or cleaners in the houses of the
whites and were paid only one or two dollars per week.
They were without any vote or method of protesting their
servitude. It was ironic that their defenders and critics had
to be courageous whites from the outside the country, like
Michael Scott, or whites from inside who consequently
were regarded as traitors to their own race, such as Alan
Paton. Both of these men were Christians in word and deed.

It took courage to defend the underprivileged and
the unprivileged, such as the Revd. Michael Scott did.
What contrasting views of him were held! For example, I
heard his former South African bishop refer to him as "a
wandering nuisance" and the black chief executive officer
of a major philanthropic foundation in New York City said
of the same Michael Scott that his stand for the Hereros in
the United Nations Organization "has persuaded millions of
my people that there is one white Christian in the world as
color-blind as his Master. He is our Good Samaritan in the
flesh."

I suppose it was because I had in a very minor way
preached and published articles advocating the rights of Africans that I was elected Chairman of the Congregational
Union of South Africa. But my conscience was so troubled

that I could not keep quiet. It was quite clear to me that Christianity implied democracy.

The article that created the greatest controversy was one I wrote entitled, " How far is South Africa a Christian Democracy?" with the subtitle "The Sword of God's eternal justice hangs threateningly over us." Initially it was an address given at the Annual Meetings of the Congregational Union of South Africa. As an article, it appeared in the widely circulated paper, *The South African Weekly*, on Friday, November 17, 1950. I may as well summarize what I wrote to convey my burning convictions. I began by pointing out that a limited democracy was first found in its Greek and Roman beginnings, and the theocracy of the Old Testament. Then I claimed that a democracy was the fruit of the Christian tradition, especially in the English Free Churches where the art of self-government was learned in the Congregational Church meetings of the seventeenth century and in the Methodist class meetings of the eighteenth century. Further I added that it was a Baptist, Roger Williams, who taught religious toleration first, and the Reformed protest for liberty was seen in the classic protest of a Huguenot to the intolerant King of France, with the clarion cry: "Sire, the Church of God is an anvil that has worn out many hammers."

In the article, there followed an analysis of the Christian foundations of Democracy, those dynamic evangelical beliefs that keep Christianity vigorous and the national conscience sensitive. I claimed first the infinite importance and sacredness of the individual. For totalitarianism, Communist or Fascist, the individual is insignificant. In the factory a "hand"; in the home a consuming unit; in elections a statistic; in war mere cannon-fodder; in industry a cog in the machine.

How utterly different is the Christian estimate of the individual! In the Bible God and man occupy the center stage of the vast cosmos. God creates man in His own image. The same man, according to the New Testament, was rescued by the Eternal Son of God who became man for his sake and was crucified for love of him. Totalitarianism reduces man to a lump of clay, whereas Communism elevates him to a fantastic high pinnacle, declaring that he will achieve the perfection of his being in the classless society. And this despite sin, suffering, and death !

By contrast, the Bible has a sobering realism in its anthropology, seeing man as both an imitator of God and a rebel against God. "The Cross" said Nathaniel Micklem "is the denial of all facile optimisms and the Resurrection of all easy pessimisms."

The second foundation of democracy, I thought, is the conception of brotherhood and sisterhood, and the equality before God which is the proof of us being children in Christ. Berdyaev summed it up by saying "Religion means Communion and Community." In the New Testament days, Christians saw that divisions were a civil war of the human race. The Church then was the parable of the Good Samaritan in action. Roman matron and slave-girl, Semite, Latin and Greek together, transcended race and class as they partook of the common cup which proclaimed that they belonged to a new race of which the Messiah was the first-born of many brethren. Our very concern for fraternity or sorority—the essence of democracy as a principle—is a recognition of Jesus Christ as Everyone's Elder Brother.

In the third place, in a true democracy the supreme virtue is compassion, literally "suffering with" people. Our truest identity with others is when we become, in the words of the poet Keats, "those to whom the miseries of the world are miseries and will not let them rest." Democracies are built neither on fear nor on force, but on trust (merely another name for faith) and the compassionate person alone is to be trusted and alone worthy to wield power.

The fourth foundation of Christian Democracy is hope, belief in human progress. The Christian tradition and Gospel gave hope to a despairing world. The hope it encouraged was not an inevitable automatic progress, as if humanity was standing on an everascending escalator—it was a progress dependent upon co-operation with God. "All things work together for those who love God."

According to Dr. Gilbert Murray all past civilizations have died from failure of nerve, for they toppled over through unjust domination and the only energetic ones left were the barbarians and slaves who had every justification for tearing down the thin fabric of civilization.

The fifth foundation of a Christian democracy is the recognition of the desperateness of original sin, and the absolute need to be God-oriented and assisted by Divine grace to overcome the *damnosa haereditas* as our profoundest theologians have called our inevitable predisposition towards evil.

Then I asked the embarrassing question: "How far is South Africa a Christian Democracy?" South Africa, I charged, had not been daringly democratic enough. In other lands the failure of democracy had been economic; class divisions had made a mockery of egalitarianism, and the Mammon of Capitalism had been allowed to defeat or postpone God's plans. In South Africa, the failure of fraternity had been racial. As Myrdal, the Scandinavian sociologist pointed out in his *American Dilemma* the problem of race is the problem in the heart of the white American who lives in a society praising democracy, but paralysed by racial discrimination, so that compassion is imprisoned, fear mounts on the shoulders of fear, and a mortal and fatty degeneration of conscience sets in. We suffer from the same disease in South Africa. The ugly truth is that we are not a Christian brotherhood but a caste society. We may be described over politely as a white aristocracy and minority, or impolitely as a black slave state. It denies Lincoln's definition of a democracy, for it is the government of a few of the people by fewer of the people in the interests of a few of the people. How can it be a democracy when 80 per cent of the populations are disinherited? Four-fifths of the population because of the pigmentation of their skin have no direct representation in Parliament. Is a country a democracy where almost 80% live in shanties where a white farmer would not allow his pedigree pigs to root? Is a nation a true democracy where skill is repressed because the color of the hands is dark, and by a nation claiming to follow the teach-

ings of Christ the Carpenter? Is there equality where the
Law apportions different penalties to different races for the
same crime?
    I finally ended with the following exhortation:

> Do you wonder that the glaring spotlight of the world's
> publicity is trained embarrassingly upon us, or that we are
> considered as the moral lepers of the modern world? We
> cloak our repressive measures with talk about "white su-
> periority". But the just, holy and compassionate Christ
> would have branded us not as white superiors, but as whit-
> ed sepulchers. We are a nation that has lost the art of com-
> passion—our tearducts are as dry as dusty river-beds after
> a drought. I believe that the sword of God's Eternal Justice
> hangs threateningly over us. History teaches us that when a
> nation or civilization tries to break the laws of God, it
> breaks itself, and is thrown on the scrap heap of God, for
> God has no further use for it.
> South Africa is at the crossroads of destiny. She is faced
> with two alternatives: either to implement her Democracy,
> ease her conscience and create the good faith between the
> races which is the only cement of a multiracial society; or,
> by further and more fearful repression to disintegrate and
> finally destroy our society.

    In March of 1951 I was able to play a small part in
the Inaugural Celebrations of Rhodes as an independent
University (no longer Rhodes University College). The
Celebrations were spread over five days, and included an
Address by the Minister of Education, Arts, and Science,
the Hon. J. H. Viljoen, a Lecture by the Principal of Bristol
University in England, Sir Philip Morris, as well as the con-
ferment of honorary Doctorates on four candidates of distinction, including two fellows of the Royal Society of London. On Sunday March 11th, there was to be a Thanksgiving Service held in the fine, neo-gothic cathedral of Grahamstown, and as the Professor of Religion it was my privilege and responsibility to preach the sermon. The theme I
chose was the correlated search for truth in Religion and

Education. I don't suppose that I shall ever have again six distinguished scientists, all Fellows of the Royal Society of London, in any congregation that I address. My choice as preacher gave me special delight since I, as a Free Church or Nonconformist minister, was preaching in a High Anglican Cathedral! The family must have been impressed by this invitation because I still possess a crayon drawing of myself done by my daughter Christine, showing me wearing the red and blue gown of the Oxford D. Phil. and my face enlarged, with huge eyes and authentic bald pate! The impact on the vast congregation was considerably less than on our five year old.

It was also during its 1951 Assembly that the Congregational Union of South Africa chose me to be Chairman-Elect. Since the African ministers and lay delegates as well as those of the Cape Colored had equal votes with the Caucasian ministers and lay delegates, I suspect it was my liberal stance on race relations that produced this election result. I was inaugurated as Chairman after my six months sabbatical leave from the University and at the famous mission station of Tiger Kloof, Bechuanaland, in 1952.

After five exhaustingly laborious and fascinating years in South Africa, I was relieved to spend six months on a sabbatical spent briefly in England, but for four months in Canada and the United States which was financed by a generous grant from the Carnegie Corporation of New York. It enabled me to study the development of teaching Divinity in universities and theological seminaries in North America. It was an immensely rewarding and invigorating experience from which I was to learn a great deal.

4

A VISIT TO NORTH AMERICA: GENERAL IMPRESSIONS

The visit to North America was a Herculean and whirlwind trip. Fortunately I kept a journal of 253 pages in which to record my impressions and many interviews or conversations with leading theological educators in both Canada and the United States. To start with, it seems appropriate to provide statistics of the mileage covered and the number of institutions I visited.

My travels from Grahamstown and back covered 27,914 miles and took me by ship from Port Elizabeth to Southampton, across the Atlantic to New York, and the same journey in reverse. The sea voyages were approximately 17,900 miles. I flew 7,541 miles on the North American Continent, and traveled 1,553 miles by train and by automobile 1,020 miles.

The universities with theological departments I visited were 22, including Harvard, Yale, Princeton, Columbia, California, Southern California, Howard, Fisk, Duke, Vanderbilt, Chicago, Northwestern, City College (then, now City University) of New York, Oberlin, Boston, Butler (Indianapolis), Drew, North Carolina and Stanford in the U.S.A. and McGill (Montreal), Queen's (Kingston) and Victoria (Toronto) all three universities in Canada.

Eleven seminaries were also visited, including Union Theological Seminary in New York City, Andover-Newton in Massachussetts, Pacific School of Religion in Berkeley, Berkeley Baptist Seminary, Chicago Theological Seminary, Episcopal Theological School in Cambridge,

Garrett Biblical Institution, Princeton Theological Seminary, Hartford Seminary Foundation, Knox Theological School (Toronto), the Presbyterian Theological College in Montreal, as well as the Religious Education and Missionary Training Center at Scarrit College in Nashville.

It now seems amazing to me that it was possible to do all that traveling on a grant of $3,000 for myself and an additional $500 to cover the expenses of my wife Brenda, for the last one of my four months. The cost was only about $20 per day for 125 days for myself, but this included a great deal of free hospitality provided by several of the institutions and Union Theological Seminary in New York City, which was my headquarters for this stay, while living in "the prophet's chambers", was especially generous to me. It was the travel and the meals which used up most of the money.

Before detailing some of the most impressive interviews I had with theological leaders in both countries I would like to give my impressions of life in North America as these were formed in 1952 and my visits to some historic sites and famous museums. Of course, the reader should be warned to discount all generalizations made about a Continent which then had a population of over 140 millions and forty-eight United States and ten Canadian Provinces which almost represented 58 different countries. The only generalization I find it safe to make is that in North America the characteristic outlook was forward-looking confidence, while South Africa was anxiously introspective, and Great Britain seemed to be looking backwards at the palmy days of its historic past. I noticed also a refreshing relative lack of class distinction, although race discrimination in the South came to almost the same thing. The U.S.A.'s greatest distinction it seemed to me was its capacity to weld a vast heterogeneous mass of immigrants from many European countries into the unity of American citizenship. However, Hispanics and Asiatics had not and have not yet been integrated in the same way.

It was also refreshing to live in a country where ability and hard labor, rather than social prestige, largely

determined the ascent of the ambitious and industrious.
While many Americans professed to envy the English their
historic monarchy above the political struggle and the pageantry that goes with it, they were prouder that the great of
our own nation were so accessible to wayfaring folk. We
witnessed how true this was in the natural way the worship-
ers at Riverside Church in Manhattan went up to shake
hands with the former five-star General Eisenhower and
wished him well for his campaign for the Presidency of the
United States. There was no apparent bodyguard to provide
the protection that hedges a potential future President.

The United States seemed by comparison with shab-
by, bomb-torn Europe, fantastically prosperous; but Americans hastened to assure me that higher salaries and wages
were reduced by the higher cost of living. But as far as food
and material comforts (including cars) were concerned,
they lived better than their transatlantic cousins. The contrast between the United States and Britain would seem to
give some point to the adage that plain living and high
thinking go together. I had it on the authority of President
Henry Z. Walck of the Oxford University Press of New
York that the 40 million Britishers read as many books as
the 120 million Americans. "But", he added," Americans
are a great magazine reading people."

If the impression has been given that the American
people are uninterested in culture, it is totally false, as their
historical, scientific and art museums, their concert halls
and theatres, and the high proportion of the population that
attends universities and colleges, all amply demonstrate.
The thoughtful among them I found to be genuinely
alarmed that Hollywood should be regarded as the cultural
embassy for the United States. However, I saw few attempts to provide films of a more meditative nature, or
even documentaries which the rest of the world requires to
understand the creative institutions in American life. Visiting the American Art and History Museums was an
astounding experience, in Boston, Chicago, New York,
Philadelphia, Washington and Los Angeles.

Among the historical museums, we were excited by

the exhibits in the Smithsonian in Washington, which included the elementary plane in which the Wright brothers flew in North Carolina and the plane in which Lindbergh flew alone across the Atlantic to France. While in the Library of Congress we saw the Gutenberg and Great Mainz Bibles of the fifteenth century. Moreover, to see the original Declaration of Independence and the Constitution framed in a glass case in solid gold seemed to give the lie to Henry Ford's assertion that "History is bunk."

Dr. John Knox, genial New Testament professor at Union Seminary in New York City, drove me to the Cloisters, which is partly the reconstruction of a Cistercian monastery, and is located near the great George Washington Bridge that crosses the Hudson River and links New York to New Jersey. Financed by the Rockefeller Foundation, the Cloisters Museum was rebuilt from ruins purchased in Southern France and Spain, and is a superb mirror of medieval architecture and art in the modern metropolis. Among the treasures we viewed were the Unicorn series of tapestries created for Anne of Britanny who twice became Queen of France. They had been long in the possession of the Rochefoucaulds. A very rare silver and gilt chalice of Antioch, an early Christian object, came from the 4th or 5th century A.D. It had a vineleaf pattern and depicted Christ and the Apostles. Finally on a sarcophagus (literally a *flesh-eater* of a coffin), in addition to the symbols denoting "Christ resurrected" there was to its left a Greek "m" and to its right a Greek "u" which, Professor Knox proposed, stood for the *monogenes uios* or "only-begotten Son." These were a minuscule part of the offerings of the Cloisters.

I was introduced to the Museum of Modern Act by a friend, a future professor of Philosophy, Mary Stewart, who was completing her Ph.D at Columbia University. There we saw a special show of the early works of Picasso and his vast mural of the Bombing of Guernica. I shall never be able to erase the memory of the contorted human forms, and the jagged saw-toothed instruments in their vivid contrast of soft flesh and hard metal. The heads jolted backwards, the writhing bodies, the staring eyes of the victims, and the mechanical heavy and brutal forms of oppression, and above all the rearing horse with dilated nostrils, made more fearful by death-dealing man, were all together a shattering image of despair created by the diabolical ingenuity of man. While there the intricate patterns of the imagined tropical forests and animals of Henri Douanier Rousseau, as also the vivid colors and subtle patterns of Henri Matisse delighted me. Seurat was Byzantine in his mosaic minuteness and so scientific was his technique that only colors differentiated his points or dots to indicate sea or sky. The most disillusioned picture I saw there was in a painting of a Jewish synagogue in Poland, where the dervish gesture of the rabbi and inane look on the faces of his boy assistants coupled with chandeliers and garish colors made it look like a dance hall. Was the painter saying: "O Lord, how long?" or even more likely "Ring down the curtain—God's earth is an empty stage and life a farce."

The spidery words in my journal cannot evoke the great joy of spending five and a half hours in Washington's National Gallery of Art. I can only list some of the items in the permanent collection that intrigued me most. Among the great Italian paintings were the Madonnas of Botticelli and Raphael, the *Crucifixion* of Perugino and Tintoretto's *Storm on the Sea of Galilee*. On the French side, I liked Cezanne's *Mill-Pool* and Edgar Manet's *Wayside Musicians*. I was also fascinated by a special exhibition of Henri de Toulouse-Lautrec, the father of modern commercial art, and particularly by one painting of two horsemen going all out in a race viewed from the rear. By contrast the delicate porcelain blue and white bas reliefs of *The Madonna and Child* of de la Robbia delighted me. Most of all, El Greco's *Enthronement of the Virgin* struck me by the vertical thrust of its mannerist elongation and the excitement of the angels surrounding her.

Among American painters, I particularly admired J. S. Copley's portraits and Gilbert Stuart's *Washington Profile*. Macy Cassatt's memorable *Three figures in the Bow of a Boat* and her portraits of women and children display the sensitivity and tenderness of this American Impressionist.

It was another Professor of New Testament Studies, Dr. Paul Minear, a future faculty member of Yale Divinity School, who conducted me to the Boston Museum of Fine Arts, and incidentally saved me from the consequence of an enthusiastic gesture of mine. We luxuriated in the Modern Art section of the Museum, where we were particularly impressed by the famous Gauguin mural *D'òu venons nous? Que sommes nous? Ou allons nous?* ("Where do we come from? Who are we? Where do we go?') Its exotic colors and triangular groupings contrasted with spider-shaped trees, and it was suffused with a sense of history disillusioning primitivism.

As always Vincent Van Gogh's contrasting colors, vigorous brushwork, and rhythmical interlinking of land, vegetation and sky delighted us in *The Ravine,* as did the portrait of his postman friend in a jolly hue of blue. I was also very pleased to see my first original Rouault, *The Clown,* with its subtle intercoloring, typical stained-glass leaden contours, and gem-like brightness. He was pathetic in his sadness since his function was to make other's laugh.

We also revelled in the satirical draughtmanship of the Rowlandson collection and admired the El Greco *Monk,* the Rubens *Moor* and the Roger Van der Weyden *Crucifixion.* The only miserable moment of this visit occurred when I made a sweeping gesture which would have toppled a miniature statue from off its pedestal, had not Paul Minear protected it. In other ways, he was also a superb host.

If my experience was in any way typical, the visitor to North America will be overwhelmed by the hospitality given in clubs, hotels and restaurants. He or she may be surprised that one is so rarely invited to their homes, though it is a more frequent occasion in Canada. This was because busy Americans seemed so rarely to eat in their own homes, and particularly in the large cities. Presumably, this is because many wives are engaged in gainful professional occupations.

The women seemed to me to be extremely well-dressed, more flamboyantly than in England, but perhaps less subtly than in France. What is even more important is that emancipation from the home (possibly purchased at the too great price of the comparative neglect of their children) and the installment of electric labor-saving devices, have enabled them to cultivate intellectual and welfare pursuits. In some cases they seemed extremely knowledgeable.

American children of the middle class seemed remarkably sophisticated as compared with their more disciplined English counterparts, whom they are taught to regard as little Lord and Lady Fauntleroys. I was told a story to illustrate this which seemed devastatingly humorous to the narrator. Apparently a teacher was recounting to her American class the story of an English boy who was dramatically rescued from shipwreck. "What do you think the English boy said on reaching the lifeboat?" asked the teacher. The Yankee boy replied: "Because he was an English boy I suppose he said: 'Thank you'." In the neighborhood of Boston we were shown a new school. Seemingly it replaced a building which had been burnt down by a small boy to spite the teacher who had crossed his inclinations. I must report truthfully that many young Americans were charming, and it seems that even some of the most undisciplined children grow into responsible and courteous adults.

American newspapers are a valuable clue to the American way of life. *The New York Times* (which on February 17th, 1952 had a Sunday News edition of 182 pages, including various magazine insets comprising an extra 120 pages) is one of the best informed in the modern world, but not many newspapers are as responsible either in their selection of news or in their commentary on it. I was surprised by the sheer provincialism or even parochialism of most newspapers in the Middle West and the South which hardly reported what was going on in Washington or in New York, so full were they of parish-pump politics. And they invade privacy at times we should consider indelicate. I saw an Indianapolis newspaper which printed a photograph of the front seat of a car which displayed the incinerated remains of a local citizen burned in an accident. I shudder to think what the impressions of his relatives would be.

Americans take their politics as seriously, and often as bitterly, as South Africans do. But I was delighted to note that they are their own most penetrating critics. Most American citizens, like bulls, have a remarkable incapacity in distinguishing pink from red in politics. And yet, some of their greatest achievements, such as the Tennessee and Missouri Valley Authorities (I had the privilege of visiting the great dams and communities of the former) are the benefits of socialization.

What makes life so zestful is that most Americans are inveterate experimenters, unimpeded by stuffed-shirt tradition, and they are a far more sober and responsible people than their overseas critics make them out to be. They are firm believers in the democratic way of life, although they have still to realize that there is an economic as well as a political side to democracy. I was most grateful for American open-heartedness, and glad that the most powerful nation on earth contained a dominantly God-fearing and church-attending people, sensitive to the needs of the underprivileged in the rest of the world, and still heedful of the ethical imperatives of the Jewish Decalog and of the Christian Gospel.

This is probably the place where I should describe the religion of the American people as I found it. There are three very great differences between the religion of Britain and the United States. First, there is almost total separation of churches and the State. There is no single dominant Church corresponding to the Church of England in England or the Church of Scotland in Scotland. Presbyterians are considerably more numerous than Congregationalists (now renamed the United Church of Christ), but they are greatly outnumbered by Baptists, Methodists, and Lutherans, and no Protestant denomination equals the Roman Catholics numerically.

Secondly, this vast country has been a haven for many persecuted religious groups, and each can spread its tenets with the full protection of the law. This also means that since no government sponsors religion, the adherents of each "faith" are fully responsible for its maintenance and mission. If you will, all churches in the United States are Free Churches. Thirdly, the mobility of the population is extremely high. One family in four moves every year. Your business executive or salesman in a mammoth company is told to move from New York to San Francisco (or Atlanta or Houston) if not at the drop of a hat then shortly after a telephone call. This leads to a rootless and restless state of mind, and so religious people often attend the nearest church, which will vary with the area they move to. A Princeton Presbyterian moving to Boston would almost certainly contact the nearest United Church of Christ, but if he were sent to Texas he would become a temporary Methodist or Baptist, and if he went to Virginia, he might become an Episcopalian. Thus there is very much more "crossing" from one denomination to another than occurs in Britain, and also much less blowing of denominational trumpets. Fifty per cent of its ministers in the United Church of Christ belonged originally to other denominations in which they were ordained.

Furthermore experimentalism, as mentioned previously, is a way of life over here. I well remember the Revd. Dr. Cecil Northcott emphasizing this point in a cautionary story. Coming off a Cunarder in New York harbor, he was met by a radio reporter who thrust a microphone in his hand with the query: "Dr. Northcott, what's new in religion in Britain?" The suave Dr. Northcott replied: "In Britain we ask, what's old and trusty and tried, not what's new." An American might suspect that what was trusty was a euphemism for what is rusty, so anti-traditional is the spirit. Is there any other land where "It's history" means "That's irrelevant"?

In 1952 the majority of the population in the United States was regularly church-going. This raises the question: "Why do Americans attend Church? Clearly, in part they go to Church for religious reasons. They wish to overcome the evil tendencies in themselves and the corruptions of society. They wish to learn how to cope with suffering and

frustration and how to overcome the fear of death. They are
looking for a vision of life with transcendent and beneficial
value in a technocratic society that has no values to offer
except grossly material ones. And in all these searches,
they are helped by a Gospel and a believing community
that provides companionship and encouragement.
But like all human beings, their motives are mixed.
They also seek social benefits from church-going. For example, in this highly mobile society it is very important for
a newcomer rapidly to establish his or her respectability
first, and a little later his or her trustworthiness. The surest
way to do this is to join a church, bringing a letter of transfer from the minister of their previous church. The proof of
final acceptance in the new church is to be appointed or
elected an office-bearer, such as being a vestryman at Holy
Trinity Episcopal, or an elder at Paradise Road Reformed.
What parent indeed is not anxious that his or her
children should meet suitable young people? Where are
they likelier to make reliable friends of their own age than
at church? The American churches are superbly organized
for all age-groups, with day kindergartens and senior citizen classes. They even have clubs for lonely widowers,
widows and divorcees in several churches, as well as for
unemployed persons. All needs are catered for.
It always seemed to me a great advantage for the
American churches that they are not socially, as the British
churches are, in competition with the public-houses or tav-
erns. The latter are natural social centers, as are European
street-cafés with their awnings sheltering from the sun.
There is no equivalent over here. Drinking is done chiefly
in hotels or homes. The churches and the Y.M.C.A.s and
the Y.W.C.A.s provide a home away from home many people so desperately need. That is one reason at least for the
social success of the churches.
It was Dean Inge of St. Paul's Cathedral, London,
who insisted that "Labels are libels." Many American
churchgoers would agree with him. Certainly in matters of
worship it is exceedingly difficult to tell the difference between one denominational worship service and another, ex-

cept for the consistent and undeviating Scripturalism of the conservative Protestants. All Protestant churches in cities have gowned choirs and printed service orders. The choirs may sing anything from *Ave Maria* to Kettleby's *Baksheesh* without any sense of incongruity, except in the larger cities where the quality of the music is equalled only by cathedral choirs in Britain. Alas, they will only leave the Protestant congregations two hymns to sing, and the congregations respond by singing them half-heartedly.

The minister, unless a Roman Catholic, an Episcopalian or a Lutheran, will rarely if ever wear a clerical collar. He will probably wear a gown, but almost never an academic hood even though he will often be a double graduate, in arts and divinity. If he is a Lutheran, or a "high" United Church of Christ minister, he will emulate the Episcopalian rector by donning a surplice. Only the use of a set liturgy will distinguish Lutherans and Episcopalians from other Protestant services. So how do you distinguish denominations in America? It would be easy to answer: "You don't; it's very confusing." But I think, and I suggest it tentatively, that you distinguish Protestant denominations politically, culturally and socially. The *avant-garde* Church politically, interracially, and sexually (in that it ordains avowed homosexuals and has a notable ministry to such) is the United Church of Christ. The *avant-garde* Churches aesthetically , as their superbly modern buildings, paraments, stained-glass and banners show, are the Episcopalians and the Lutherans. The former are more liberal theologically than the latter. The socially "upper-crust" denominations are the Episcopalians and the Presbyterians. Their leading members will be high executives in industry and commerce and they will also be part of the "cocktail set".

While officially there is a complete separation between Church and State, in practice this has been breached in several ways. Studies made by sociologists and church historians have emphasized that there is in the United States what is termed a "civil religion". Its characteristic is to dilute doctrine by affirming only what different denominations, and in some cases what different monotheistic religions hold in common. It is almost a return to America's religion of the eighteenth century, Deism, which a Presbyterian theologian of the previous century, John Howe, summarized as believing: "There shall be a God provided he does not interfere." It was borrowed from Voltaire and Paine and developed through its own American Ethan Allen. It is evident on important public occasions, such as the inauguration of a new President, when it is customary to have prayers or lessons of Scripture read by representatives of the Catholic, Protestant and Jewish faiths. It is also exhibited at the graduation exercises of universities and schools, when the clergyman must avoid embarrassing anyone by making distinctive faith claims. In the armed forces, there are inevitably representatives of different denominations appointed in proportion to the strengths of their religious communities, but since smaller religious groups will be rarely represented, there is a growing ecumenism, and possibly even an increasing Deism.

Historically, however, credit must be given to the extraordinary activism shown by leaders of the religious communities. This alone can explain the vigorous weekday as well as Sunday life in the churches. The amazing fact is that, although the United States has been involved in three major wars during this century, the vast majority of its liberal clergymen have been and continue to be committed pacifists. But two other immensely important factors account for the continuing impact of religion on society, each of which deserves some detailed consideration. One is the role that religion plays among religious minorities, and the other is the very significant contribution of the "Social Gospel" especially among Protestants.

The "spirituals"—those comforting affirmations of musical creeds devised by the African-Americans to console themselves in the days of slavery, together with the more recent song associated with Martin Luther King, "We shall overcome"—are a proof of how deeply religion has not only provided encouragement to the victims of exploitation, but given them in their own churches a freedom and responsibility they were not allowed to exercise in the out-

side world. The best study of the compromises of the dominantly white churches is still H. Richard Niebuhr's *The Social Sources of Denominationalism*, which justifiably pillo-
ries the limitations of the Caucasian Christians in their half-
hearted attempt to love their black neighbors, but it also
demonstrates the vigor of the black churches and their
members and the sincerity of their faith and life.

The most cogent proof of the important influence of
religion on society in America is the still significant impact
of the "Social Gospel". Now over a century old, it attempted to combine the politico-economic insights of socialism
with the motivations of Christianity, much as F. D. Maurice
and his Christian Socialists had done in Victorian England.
The significant theological difference, however, was that
for the Christian Socialists the Incarnation was the pivotal
doctrine, while for the Social Gospelers the vaguer Kingdom of God was the primary focus.

The major historian of this phenomenon is C. Howard Hopkins and his study is entitled, *The Rise of the Social Gospel in American Protestantism, 1865-1915* published in 1940. The Social Gospel was an important attempt
to demonstrate the relevance of the Christian faith and to
redefine the role of the churches in the acute political, economic and industrial crises marking the last decade of the
nineteenth and the first of the twentieth century. The most
theologically sophisticated expositor of the Social Gospel
was a Baptist minister and theological professor, Walter
Rauschenbusch. His often cited aphorisms distinguish between the church as an introverted worshipping community
and the Kingdom of God as the expression of social justice
in daily life. "The Church," he wrote, "is primarily a fellowship for worship; the Kingdom is a fellowship for righteousness." In the same book, *Christianity and the Social
Crisis*, he also claimed that "the Kingdom of God breeds
prophets, the Church breeds priests and theologians. The
Church runs to tradition and dogma; the Kingdom of God
rejoices in forecasts and boundless horizons."

This theology was defective in overstressing the im-
manental conception of God while depreciating the Divine

transcendence in its demand for corporate ethics while ne-
glecting the need for personal transformation and disciple-
ship. It was also inadequate in its too evolutionary interpretation of the key category—the Kingdom of God, and its
undervaluing of the institutional Church with its sacramental life. Its strength was as a theology that issued in vigorous action.

It produced churches in the great urban centers that
provided food and drink for the poor and the homeless, and
helped to get them jobs, and even prepared the indigent for
the jobs that were available. It motivated thousands of well-
heeled men and women to take up careers in social work.
The Social Gospel even revolutionized public piety in the
Protestant worship services. Rauschenbusch's contribution
here was monumental through the widespread influence of
his book, *For God and the People: Prayers for the social
Awakening* (1910). In that volume there are prayers for categories of people previously unremembered before God,
such as firemen, policemen and children forced to work.
His holy anger is white hot in the prayer "Against the Ser-
vants of Mammon" as he recalls those "who grind down the
strength of workers by merciless toil and fling them aside
when they are mangled and torn and "who paralyze the
hand of justice by corruption and blind the eyes of the people with lies." These prayers created a new devotional cur-
rency in Protestantism.

The same was true of the impact of hymnody inspired by the Social Gospel. Jay T. Stocking, a Congregationalist, wrote a hymn with the opening line "O Master-
workman of the race" finding in the Carpenter of Nazareth
empathy for the artisans of the time, but the most successful hymn of this theme was Henry Van Dyke's "They who
tread the path of labor." This Presbyterian divine avoided
the peril of a reduced Christology, insisting on the divinity
as well as the humanity of Christ, and urging that all who
work should bear their family responsibility, as Jesus did
for his widowed mother, brothers and sisters, and also ab-
sorb his sacrificial spirit, and live in constant companionship with the Divine Father. One is, however, left wonder-

ing how many trade unionists would sing the lines:

> They who work without complaining
> Do the holy will of God.

A Methodist minister, Frank Mason North, wrote a noble hymn of the Social Gospel which began "Where cross the crowded ways of life." Its vivid compassion mirrors the overcrowding, the interracial animosities, the burdened wives, and the pallid children of the New York City that he knew and served so well. He heard the call of Christ who came down from the mountain of Transfiguration to the valley of crowded need sounding again "above the noise of selfish strife." One of the latest and probably the best hymn of this type was Fosdick's superb "God of grace, and God of glory." The Social Gospel movement both in its intercessory prayers and in its stirring social hymns awakened the social conscience of Protestantism in America.

Even when theological neo-orthodoxy succeeded the Social Gospel, the new theology maintained the old ethical corporate imperatives. This was seen in Reinhold Niebuhr's famous *Leaves from the Notebook of a Tamed Cynic* which mirrors his experience as a minister in the nation's automobile capital, Detroit in Michigan, where several members of his congregation were employed by the Ford Motor Company. He saw them turned, from persons into "hands" as a consequence of mass-production factory methods, without any sense of their contribution to the whole, and they were discontinued like rusty tools if through ill health or age they could no longer meet the minimum production schedules. Niebuhr's subsequent writings and the influential magazine, which he co-edited, *Christianity and Crisis* continued to bring a Christian critique of depth and relevance to the industrial and technocratic society of his time.

The contribution of religion to the improvement of society was never as powerful in the United Kingdom as it was in the United States both because the church attendance was a much smaller fraction of the population as a whole, and because the impressive exponents of Christian social ethics were in the major university-related theological seminaries in the United States, chief among them the Union Theological Seminary in New York City where Reinhold Niebuhr became professor of Applied Christianity, and Yale Divinity School where his brother Richard taught the same subject.

My all too brief survey and contrast of religion in the United States and the United Kingdom leads to the following conclusions. The greater continuing impact of religion in the United States may be attributed to the following clusters of causes. First, here was no exclusive, dominating, established Church, but all churches were encouraged and had to do their own vigorous missionary work to consolidate and expand their influence. Secondly, apart from their primary spiritual function, the churches have attracted their members by the social and educational needs they serve. Thirdly, the impressive experimentalism of the American ethos kept the churches in the United States thoroughly up-to-date in their thinking and planning, and the vast size and varied provisions of the churches in the major cities has to be seen to be believed. Fourthly, the recognition that America was an ever-open door for the persecuted has led to the vigor and variety of religion in the United States. Fifthly and finally, the democratic character of American life has encouraged non-hierarchical churches to flourish in the U.S.A. So it is not in the least surprising that it is here that independent and autonomous local churches, allowing the maximum opportunity for local government and initiative, have flourished better than anywhere else in the world. It was a profound privilege to see many of these churches in active service during my visit in 1952.

Finally, as I reflect on my North American experiences, I cannot forget the impression made upon me by dramatic scenery and historical sites. Since the Niagara Falls are hemmed in on the South side by the United States and on the North side by Canada, it was the first dramatic scene that I saw. The visit was special also because I was accompanied by my only relative on this continent—Uncle Gwilym, my father's brother—whom I had contacted by phone in Toronto, only because I made out a G. Davies in a Canadian list of addresses, in a New York library weeks before. He and his wife drove me from Toronto to Niagara Falls.

It was not as dramatic as I expected it to be, because it was in the first week of March. On this visit, there was no vegetation in the environs, but only snow, frost and icicles; and I could not see the full spate of the Horseshoe Falls from the green at the upper level to the foaming green-white cauldron below, which I saw in a second visit from the American side. This side of the Falls gave the impression that Americans had said: "Let us build hotels as high as the Falls, to show that we are as smart as the Creator or the geologists." And they did; but they aren't!

My first visit to the Canadian side of the Niagara Falls let me see the Gorge with several vast waterfalls, as the hotels were smaller than on the American side. The rapids rush madly down to the Horseshoe Falls (interrupted only by several rocks and the hulk of a bootlegging ship), where there is a very wide and sheer drop. The thundering green water explodes in the whirlpool below and sends up a shower of what looks like steam to a height of approximately 50 feet above the Falls. What could be seen of the American side from the Canadian side indicated that part of the Falls was frozen and it appeared like gigantic stalactites over the rim of the basin. Down below vast rocks looked like snowy sea-anemones created by a gigantic Neptune for his grandchildren. It was undoubtedly a memorable sight and site, and this geological fault or Divinely-created wonder exceeded the expectation.

Another visit to a historic scene failed to live up to expectation. This was a trip to see Plymouth Rock which commemorates the landing of the first Pilgrims on the "Mayflower". This was the first settlement in New England in 1620 after a frightening sea voyage made in a very small ship, by men, women and children who sought to worship God with Scriptural simplicity and freedom, which the

Church and State in England then forbade. As a Congregationalist, I was excited at the thought of seeing where these proto-Congregationalists had landed. I was disappointed by it being "ye olde Strattefordized" like Shakespeare's English town. But historically trained eyes can see through even the ugly monument to the Pilgrims whom it is meant to honor, and through the *rock* (which the Dames of America have caged, presumably for safety) and very small and inoffensive it is. Even the Pilgrim Church is Unitarian now, though the Pilgrims were all Trinitarians!

In Pilgrim Hall, Plymouth, there was a scale model of the ship. It was only 90 feet long with a beam of 26 feet and carried 102 persons across the Atlantic, itself a saga of faith and hope.

Some compensation for my disappointment was viewing the reconstruction of an early pilgrim house in unpainted wood and thatched roof, with a barricade to keep out Indians, I suppose, although they had found them most friendly at first. They had even made a treaty with Massasoit, the Great Sachem of the Wampanoags, and the great preserver of the Pilgrims. I was also delighted to see the earliest extant house, built by the Pilgrims in 1666 and restored in 1961. This was a double-storeyed house with glass windows (not mere openings in the wood as in the earliest domiciles) which also had a tiled roof and brick chimneys. The National Monument to the Forefathers exhibited successively in bas-reliefs the Embarkation of the Mayflower, the Landing at Plymouth, the Treaty with Massasoit, and the theocratic Compact of the community of pilgrims.

From the East to the West Coast was a total contrast. I cannot hope to depict the beauty of the California shore with its bays reflecting brilliant sunshine, and I was greatly attracted to the cities of San Francisco, Berkeley, and Palo Alto in the North. The latter two housed the famous campus of the University of California, and that of Stanford University. But first I wanted to see a natural wonder, namely, the magnificent Grand Canyon. To approach it, I flew approximately 1600 miles from Nashville, Tennessee over the States of Missouri, Oklahoma, New Mexico, Colorado and Arizona and crossed two time zones until we reached Phoenix. Flying at 18,000 feet with excellent visibility we could see below largely uncultivated land, with occasional rivers and reservoirs, and vast tracts of desert.

On the 16th of May, 1952, I reached my hotel and found the temperature 70 degrees at 11 p.m. and thoroughly South African. I was wakened the next morning at 5.30 a.m. to catch the plane from Phoenix airport at 6.15 a.m. which stopped at Prescott on its way to Flagstaff. We passed over pine forests and in the near distance viewed the snow-crested Mount San Francisco (12,000 feet), the highest peak in the West. From Flagstaff I was driven in a Ford V-8 because a strike kept the Greyhound bus from operating. This car took me through the Kaibab National Forest to Bright Angel Point, where Grand Canyon itself begins. I reached there at 11.30 a.m. and caught the first stupendous view of the Canyon, its dramatically steep side revealing many different types of rocks and vegetation.

Its area is 1,008 square miles. It is 56 miles long and contains 105 miles of the Colorado River. It was produced by six shifts of volcanic activity and by erosion contributed by river, snow, rain and wind. The great chasm measured by river course is 217 miles long and varies from 4 to 18 miles wide. The bottom of the Canyon is 2500 feet above sea level, and about 4,500 feet below the South rim and 5,700 feet below the North rim. In the Grand Canyon one can see six of the seven climatic belts, ranging from the Mexican desert at the Canyon base to the Arctic-Alpine type of the San Francisco peaks. The tropical belt alone is missing .

Five Indian tribes lived in the Reservation then with about 600 families—the Hopi, Navajo, Harasupai, Paiute and Hualpai. They subsisted by creating silverware, jewelry, pottery and exquisite mats, all with Indian symbols and designs. They were sold at most modest prices. For example, I bought four Yemez brightly colored pots at 30 cents each, and two rings (one of Wyoming Jade set in silver for

$4.00, with a tax of 20%, and a ring with a sun symbol in turquoise rays, including tax for approximately $10.00.

My words cannot convey the majesty of the view as it descends for about a mile below, with its variegated hues of blue, pink, gold and brown, into the depths, all melting into each other. One can only imagine how exquisite it must be viewed by the moonlight.

A complete but interesting contrast to the Grand Canyon was my visit to Los Angeles and to Hollywood. It seems that in Los Angeles all the angels have lost their haloes. The humid atmosphere, though not the vast population and the wildly rushing traffic, resembled South African Durban. I asked a New York City taxi-driver operating there if this was an artificial or phony city. "Sure", he said "it's a Dreamer's City—they come; they don't make good, and they go back and say they did." I also gathered from the same informant that people pretended to be mature if teenagers, kids if in the middle-forties, and that borrowed names, borrowed cars, and borrowed cash (credit) was the order of the day in Celluloid City. It is also a city of ethnic variety, with African-Americans, American Indians, Hispanics, Japanese and Chinese.

I was glad to worship at "The Church of All Nations"—a Methodist Church in Los Angeles. The attendance was not high, because it was the Sunday after Easter, so there were about forty persons present including fifteen in the choir, and they were Blacks, Whites and Hispanics. One attractive feature of the service was the Offertory, which encouraged persons to make special extra contributions if they had special reasons for gratitude. One African American produced a gift for his birthday, and Dr. and Mrs. McKibben in a similar manner celebrated their twenty-five years as leaders of this congregation. The sermon, preached by an ex-Korean medical missionary, Dr. Van Buskirk, lasted thirty-two minutes. It referred to Christ's Resurrection and its triple points were: Christ lives; We shall live; and Are we worthy of immortal life? The application was very direct, asking whether we want to be like Christ, or Rockefeller, or Joe Louis the boxer, or Livingstone, or

Schweitzer, or Mary Moffatt? I was glad that there was such a community-church in Los Angeles.

The next day I went on an organized three-hour tour of film studios and the exteriors of the homes of the film stars of Hollywood. The stars and their underlings worked hard, with all the "retakes" required of them. The really successful stars alone can afford to buy the land and the vast houses which are built upon it. Each house must have had 14 to 18 rooms to furnish. We saw the house of Bing Crosby, the moderate house of Bob Hope which showed that the famous wisecracker had a sense of proportion, and the mansions of Shirley Temple, Gary Cooper, Anna May Wong and Will Rogers, of Charles Laughton on a headland over Santa Monica and of Rita Hayworth and Jane Russell and many more. We also noted the home of Eddie "Rochester" Anderson, which had to be sublet to a Caucasian, because, being an African-American, he was excluded.

Our wisecracking limousine driver said that Shirley Temple and her husband loathed publicity so much that they drove around Hollywood in a 1941 car, with battered fenders, and she wore slacks, a scarf, and dark glasses. His gossip included the comment that Gary Cooper, the assumed symbol of marital fidelity was being sued by his own wife for a divorce "on the farce of mental cruelty."

The same informant told us that Anna May Wong had to retire from films because her voice did not suit talkies, and that Will Rogers, the Mayor of Beverley, would have made a great politician. He said the immortal words: "I never saw a man I could hate." On being shown the interior of the excellent ranch home of Rogers, I entered the library, saw the bookshelves, and noted the names of two adjacent books I could make out, which were "Swastika" and "Hosses." On the whole the houses were more modest and attractive than I had expected, and their lawns, their geraniums and ivy were superbly kept, so that their gardens looked like miniature public parks for neatness and varied hues. Los Angeles citizens are less impressed by film stars and their homes and lives than the gawking visitors from the East and mid-West. Those nearer the social gods and goddesses see the clay feet and in newsprint read "What the Valet Saw"!

Our driver, asked by a passenger if thousands of girls liked to flock hopefully to Los Angeles, replied: "Yea, but not so many now. They got a raise to $14.50 a day, but they spend their time mainly if girls in restaurants, if men as taxi-drivers."

Some superb films have come out of Hollywood, the work of excellent script writers, of gifted producers and directors, and of extremely capable actors and actresses. Among the more memorable films I saw while in the United States were: the de Mille spectacular *Quo Vadis?*, Arthur Miller's book filmed as *Death of a Salesman*, and Alan Paton's book filmed as *Cry, the Beloved Country*.

The gratitude that I felt at the wonder of God's creation in the Grand Canyon, as at the Niagara Falls, remains with me today as I consider the time that so many American theologians and professors gave so readily to my requests for information and accomodation, and which made my lengthy visit such a mine of information and stimulus. The Americans are a generous and exceedingly hard-working people, as many later years in their midst have confirmed for me, and I am, I hope, their grateful debtor. One can recognize generosity by contrast. I do not believe that a famous theological institution, such as Union Seminary in New York City would have had a British counterpart that would invite a thirty-six year old visitor from South Africa hitherto unknown to them, to stand in as a substitute for Reinhold Niebuhr as a preacher at Union's Sunday service. Yet this is what they did for me on March 2nd, 1952. That indeed, is characteristic of America's faith in the future!

5

VISITING THEOLOGICAL CENTERS IN NORTH AMERICA.

Perhaps the greatest surprise for the visitor is to discover the vast size of the buildings and congregations of so many city churches. On my first day in America I was taken to Riverside Church in Manhattan and at lunch there introduced to its minister, the successor of the famous Harry Emerson Fosdick, whose name was Robert J. McCracken. He came from a Scottish Baptist Church via the Chair of Theology and Philosophy of Religion at McMaster University in Canada. In this vast neo-Gothic cathedral-like church, they can accomodate 2,500 persons as well as another 1500 in extra chapels and assembly halls. Dr. McCracken's preaching was notable for its systematic exposition of Christian doctrine and its practical relevance. He preached what he called "life-situation" sermons and he was particularly fond of using literary illustrations.

In addition to Dr. McCracken Riverside had three other ministers. Dr. Ivar Hellstrom was famous as the head of the skyscraper church school and the weekday kindergarten school. Dr. Norris Tibbets directed the pastoral work of the church, which was divided into 75 different zones with 130 zone leaders. Zone meetings were held in apartments in a given neighborhood or at the Fellowship Dinner which I had attended. The fourth minister on the Church staff was Dr. Gordon Chamberlain, who was responsible for Riverside's work among students, for Columbia is virtually on its doorstep. Riverside also had a full-time business manager with a maintenance and operating staff of 35. The

budget for Riverside Church in 1952 was a total of $522,
328 of which $147,502 was income from the endowment
largely made possible by Rockefeller benefactions. One unusual source of income was the $9,700 received from sight-
seers viewing the city's panorama from the church's 20th
storey tower with its carillon of 72 bells! The rest was to be
provided mainly from 2,298 subscribers, 450 of whom
lived more than 50 miles from New York City, and more
than 700 subscribers who were not even members of the
church

I found Dr. McCracken a most unassuming man for
the high position he held and I valued two pieces of advice
he gave me. One followed my telling him that I would soon
be going to Emmanuel College of Victoria University in
Canada to give a set of lectures on the Modern Liturgical
Movement. He said "Yes, Liturgy needs to be stressed, but
now so much time has to be spent on preparing the worship
that the sermon is often neglected. Didn't P. T. Forsyth call
the Word of God the Protestant equivalent of the Roman
Mass?" He then proceeded to give me some useful practical
advice: "You'll have to husband your dollars carefully.
Englishmen tend to overtip. Go first thing tomorrow, and
get a minister's railway concession card." He was a kindly
and sincere man. Until this meeting I had no idea of the
spectacular size of large city churches in the United States.
Frankly, I wondered how much sense of community would
be created in so huge a congregation, but there was no way
of missing the great organizational capacity of American
ministers.

Dr. McCracken was a man of middle height, fine
profile, dark hair, and sensitive eyes lightening as he
quipped. His voice had a firm, conviction-ringing tone, and
he seemed to have none of the tricks of the preacher who
played to the gallery. His success in maintaining large congregations was due to several factors. In the first place, he
asked the fundamental questions and attempted to answer
them. It is significant that his first volume of sermons was
entitled *Questions People Ask,* also the gift of his predecessor Harry Emerson Fosdick. But Dr. McCracken did not

give exactly the same answers as his predecessor nor were his illustrations drawn so commonly from case-books. His sermons were more theological in content, enlivened with poetical illustrations, and they marched relentlessly from point to point in a careful structure. Perhaps the basic difference between Fosdick and McCracken was that the former was more prophetic in his outlook and could always be counted on the side of lost causes which he persuaded his people to believe in. The only criticism I heard was not of him but of his congregation. A visitor said in my hearing: "I'd be scared to put anything less than a dollar note in the collection-plate."

About a week later, I had the privilege of meeting two superb theological administrators, Dr. Henry Pitney Van Dusen, President of Union Theological Seminary in New York City and Dr. John Bennett, Professor of Christian Ethics, who had spent three years reading theology at my old Oxford College, and would eventually become President at Union Seminary. This interview is best reported in Question and Answer terms.

> **First Question**: What are the seminal books in U.S. theology?
>
> **Answer**: Robert Calhoun, *God and the Common Life*: Kenneth Scott Latourette, *The History of the Expansion of Christianity* (7 volumes) Reinhold Niebuhr, *The Nature and Destiny of Man* (2 volumes) Paul Tillich, *Systematic Theology*, vol. 1 (eventually 3).

The first two volumes were produced by authors teaching at Yale University Divinity School, and the last two by professors at Union. Other significant theologians were said to be Wilhelm Pauck, John Mackay, Paul Minear and Daniel Day Williams. Chicago they thought was the leading center for Church historians. The historians there included Jaroslav Pelikan, James Hastings Nichols, and Martin Marty.

Second question: What are the teaching conditions for members of Union Seminary Faculty?

The answer: Retiral at 65; an assistant professor teaches for 2 sets of 3 years, an Associate professor 2 sets of 5 years. A professor teaches 7 hours a week as well as supervising theses for higher degrees. Sabbaticals are given for half a year at full pay or a year at half-salary.

Third question: What are the most popular fields for doctoral research at Union?

The answer: Theology, Philosophy of Religion, and Old Testament (the latter due to the popularity of Professor Muilenburg)

Fourth question: What proportion are B.D.s and doctoral candidates?

The answer: 250 B.Ds. who undertake basic courses for one and a half years and undertake a thesis in their final year; 150 do research work including 30 taking an Ed. D. degrees.

Fifth question: Dollars permitting, what are your plans for the future development of Union Seminary?

The answer: 1. A lay school for the training of Church leaders in New York and environs. 2. An Extension Institute for assisting ministers. 3. Correspondance Tuition in Theology. 4. More travelling professorships to enable faculty to visit Younger Church centers. 5. To increase Lending Library facilities. 6. An Institute of Graduate Studies in Theology.

Sixth Question: What is the financial structure of Union Seminary?

The answer was provided by three comparative tables:

	1916-17	1937-38	1951-52
Annual Budget	$291,000	$518,671	$1,096,431
Endowment:	$280,000	$348,000	$ 398,350
Student fees:	$ 7,500	$ 81,288	$ 228,895
Self sustaining services:	$ 500	$ 78,383	$ 259,602
Annual gifts:	$ 3,000	$ 11,000	$ 209,584
Student enrollment:	270	371	634

At a subsequent interview with Dr. Van Dusen, he

told me that he considered the most significant theological centers in the United States were Yale Divinity School and Union Theological Seminary (tactfully, he wouldn't say which was the more important of the first two.) He added to the list The Federated Faculty of Theology at Chicago and at Berkeley, California, The Pacific School of Religion and its neighbors (including Episcopal, Baptist, and Roman Catholic Seminaries). He thought that in Canada Emmanuel College—the theological College of Victoria University in Toronto—and McGill University Divinity School were the most important in the North Land .

My next important interview in New York City was with Dr. Douglas Horton who was the Minister and Secretary of the Congregational Churches in the U.S.A. Being a Congregational minister myself, it was important to meet the most important Congregationalist in the world who was able to suggest important contacts that I might make. He was a man of decision and charm and was the first theologian in the United States to translate a book by Karl Barth entitled *The Word of God and the Word of Man,* hence-warmly welcoming the neo-orthodoxy of Karl Barth. He believed in the democratic structure of Congregationalism and in its powerful interracial witness. In fact, he told me that he worshipped in a church that was predominantly black. His hope for the future was to develop Councils of professionals who could make a united witness in all kinds of specialized vocations.

He had recently bought several seventeeth century classics of English Puritanism or Congregationalism, such as the very influential Westminster *Directory of Public Worship of 1644,* which suggested topics for prayers but left ministers free to phrase them under the inspiration of the Holy Spirit. He also bought two books by the only Puritan Dean of Christ Church at Oxford University, John Owen. This lively man took me to lunch at his club where the conversation continued. He informed me that the leading Congregational historians were Drs. Fagley, Roland Bainton and Matthew Spinka. He expressed the conviction that American Congregationalism had recovered its liturgi-

cal heritage; its next task was to recover its doctrine and
polity .

At lunch he introduced me to Dr. Henry Smith
Leiper, Associate Secretary of the World Council of Chul
ches, a man who had travelled round the world 59 times,
and was full of droll anecdotes. He recounted that when he
was shown round Duke University in North Carolina at
Durham (renamed after a tobacco magnate) an African
American pointing to the tomb of this tobacco king said:
"This is Mr. Dook's cigar-fungus!" (sarcophagus). When I
happened to meet him a second time the same evening at
Englewood, New Jersey, he was most complimentary about
my article, "Faith and Fear in South Africa." which appeared in the current issue of *Christianity and Crisis.*

He told me that Congregationalists pioneered several Black universities which were now interdenominational,
including Howard University in Washington, and Fisk University in Nashville, Tennessee, both of which I visited later. As an example of the improvement in race relationships
that had taken place in America in his life-time (he was 61
years old), he instanced that his parents' families had fought
on either side of the Civil War, but that he as President of
the American Missionaries' Association, had been present
at the retiral dinner of the President of Fisk University at
which nine blacks who attended were listed in "Who's Who
in America."

I had also the privilege of interviewing the President
of the oldest and most important Presbyterian Theological
Seminary at Princeton in New Jersey, some 55 miles from
Manhattan. He was the well-known Dr. John Mackay,
Chairman of the International Missionary Council, and a
distinguished ecumenist. He outlined his theological views
to me. Truth, he said, is four square and has four balanced
aspects. First there is Revelation—the doctrinal aspect.
Then there is the Encounter with God—experience and
worship. Thirdly, there is the Community of God—the institutional. And last, Obedience—the Ethical. Absolutize
any of these aspects, he added, and you have idolatry. In
the interview he stressed that the Seminary was in the great

evangelical tradition, though not literalist; that it belonged to the largest Presbyterian Church in the world; that it had 49 different denominations represented in the student body, but of which 80% were Presbyterrians. Its distinctive chairs were those of Ecumenics (which he held) and Missions. I was impressed by Princeton Seminary's theologians, including Drs. Mackay, Paul Lehmann, George Hendry and Otto Piper. Here I was able also to attend Yale professor H. Richard Niebuhr's lecture on "Faith and knowledge"— which was an example of beautiful intellectual wrestling!

My Canadian trip took place early in March where Toronto was my first city to visit. I was delivering at Emmanuel College of the Victoria University of Toronto a set of lectures on "Twentieth Century Developments in Protestant Worship." This theological college produced the men who wrote the admirable ecumenical *Canadian Book of Common Order*, as I was informed by Principal Dawson Matheson. Dr. Hugh Matheson, a Church historian, clearly inspired the then Principal of Emmanuel, Dr. Richard Davidson, to become the virtual architect, assisted in part by Matheson and John Dow. In T*he Living Church,* subtitled *A book in Memory of the Life and Work of Rev Richard Davidson . . . Principal of Emmanuel College. Toronto (1949)* Dr. John Dow has written:

> The Book of Common Order is above all else his monument. To that task he brought his unique knowledge of the historic symbols, a reverence for the ancient tradition, a sense of the music of words and of the doctrinal realities they express, and above all an awareness that it was a living power and presence that communicated itself under the form and ritual of the Church that is His Body.

The achievement was greatly needed because the tradition in most Methodist and Presbyterian Churches, as well as in the minority Congregational Churches that joined to form the United Church of Canada was that of free or extemporary prayer. It was in the same Emmanuel College that another outstanding historian of worship was trained by Dr. Richard Davidson, namely, Professor W. D. Maxwell, who was to succeed me as Professor of Divinity at Rhodes University. His *Outline of Christian Worship* was the first ecumenical history of the developments of worship to appear in English, and has had a wide and continuing sale as well as a powerful influence.

In Toronto I had the benefit of two very illuminating interviews. My first informant was Dr. Gordon Sisco, the Secretary of the United Church of Canada. He outlined the history of the United Church, pointing out that at the beginning of the century when the Western Prairies opened up there was a movement from West to East in Canada and a Northern movement from the U.S.A. up into Canada, and it seemed that such a migration could best be served not by denominations but by a national type of Church. In 1925 the Methodists came into the union fully, and all but three Congregational churches, though Congregationalism was small, and one-third of the Presbyterians stayed out. Why did the latter take place? Dr. Sisco's explanation was "They said that union would cause them to lose the Westminster Confession of Faith as their doctrinal standard, but they were basically imperialistic, unadaptable, and wanting to retain the British connection."

I asked him to describe the current problems of the United Church of Canada. He felt that chiefly the increasing industrialization of Canada caused the population to move into metropolitan cities and asked: "Has any Protestant Church the genius to stay in the city and not become merely suburban? Roman Catholics and Anglicans with a parish system are most successful in this type of parochial work. Protestants, being middle class, move to suburbs and leave the center. Then the millenarian and Pentecostal sects buy up the abandoned Protestant city centers and make them work." He added that the day of the spell-binding minister was over, and the best ministers for this task are those who are from the people and untamed by theological training." (This was a hard kick!) He concluded: "But parish ministers will succeed and those who create community centers."

He also felt that provincialism had taken over in too many regions of Canada. There were, for example, in his view far too many theological colleges in the United Church, eight in all. Each had been attracted naturally to a university campus. It would, he said, be unreasonable to expect British Columbia to give up its seminary on the Western seaboard, but there seemed little point in having two theological colleges in the Prairie Provinces, like those in Manitoba and Saskatoon. He felt that an important ecumenical experiment was taking place at McGill University in Montreal where a federated theological faculty has members of the United Church of Canada combining with the Church of England in Canada. Later I would see this for myself.

Dr. Sisco ended this lengthy and informative interview by estimating the chances for further union in Canada. His hope was that the Church of England in Canada would be united with the United Church of Canada. He insisted that conversations between them must be maintained because they are the largest Protestant communions in Canada and the United Church of Canada is committed to be a *uniting* Church. Dr. Sisco also felt that the churches must imitate the informality, cheerful friendliness, and faith-healing, as well as the uncomplicated Gospel which most of the sects offer, but combined with a parish-type ministry.

McGill University's newly constituted Faculty of Divinity was all that Dr. Sisco projected it would be. Divinity Hall was an impressive three-storey building. The panelled hallway had excellent facsimile portraits in oils illustrating British Protestant Cooperation, with John Keble, William Tyndale, Isaac Watts, John Knox, John Wesley, John Bunyan, George Fox, William Booth, Richard Hooker. (There were, however, no Roman Catholics or any distinguished Canadians). The fine chapel displayed an Open Bible and a Cross on the altar, and dominating the whole was a splendid window designed by Strachan, representing the ascending Christ commissioning the disciples to maintain the work of the ministry. The Christ figure is colored in lemon and similar light tints, the crowds in purples, and the blues are massed heavily together for contrast. On the walls are the shields of the British Universities, a modern Orthodox Greek icon, and a polished stone from the island of Iona.

It was a particular pleasure for me to come to McGill in Montreal because my contemporary at Mansfield was Dr. George Caird, the New Testament professor, who in later years would become the first Nonconformist in the 20th century to hold an Oxford university theological chair, after being Principal of Mansfield College. Other distinguished faculty members were Dr. Robert B. Y. Scott, professor of Old Testament, who later became my great friend and golfing partner at Princeton University; Dr. Wilfred Cantwell Smith taught Comparative Religion and would later occupy a Harvard chair in this field; finally Dr. R. H. L. Slater was the professor of Systematic Theology and also the Principal of the Anglican Diocesan College. The Dean was James Sutherland Thompson, who taught the Philosophy and Psychology of Religion and had been President of Saskatchewan University and Chairman of the Canadian Broadcasting Company. I was told that he had the wisdom of a serpent combined with more than a dash of innocence. He introduced me to all his colleagues and provided useful contacts.

His interview was also exceedingly informative. He began by pointing out that the Protestant community was about 10% of the Province of Quebec, and that some 20% of the total Protestant community lived in or near Montreal. The negotiations to join the Anglican and United Church of Canada theological colleges were very tricky, especially in dealing with the Anglicans. Dean Thompson told me that a wily layman, Birks, also a very successful businessman, said: "You Anglicans use T.M. Lindsay in Church History and Hugh Mackintosh in Theology, both Presbyterians, there's no reason why you shouldn't cooperate."

The same man, after the end of the Second World War collected in post-war "conscience money" $1,500,000 (of which it is estimated he provided half) and this was the essential endowment for the future Divinity Faculty at

McGill. The arrangement was that there would be two university chairs, Philosophy of Religion and Comparative Religion, to which the university made the appointments. There were also the four fundamental chairs in Old and New Testament, Systematic Theology and Church History, which were filled by representatives of the Churches meeting with McGill's representatives. In addition the denominational colleges were preserved, since they are responsible for practical training for the ministry in their own colleges. Thus they avoid remoteness from church life. It was pointed out to me that this could only happen in a privately endowed University such as McGill is. Toronto University, for example, received its major support from the Provincial Government and inevitably requests would be made for the support of Roman Catholic and Jewish faculty and students. (American universities would think that a very good thing!)

On the lighter side Dean Thompson took me to the Faculty Club for lunch, and there I learned about the famous McGill humorist, Stephen Leacock, who taught Economics. He and his wife had a tragic life, both dying of cancer and their child was a dwarf. My informant, Professor Carruthers, thought that *Sunshine Sketches* was Leacock's finest book. He also told of when he and Leacock were staying at a lakeside cottage. He had bought bottles of whisky, beer and liqueurs and one loaf when Leacock commented: "Why waste all that money on food?

Carruthers was himself a most amusing man and told us a great story ridiculing so-called progressive education. A modern teacher saw a puddle in front of the classroom doorway. Not wanting to give the child a guilt complex, she told the children to shut their eyes and then the person who'd puddled could clear it up. All eyes were closed and they heard pit, pit, pit to the door, and pit pit pit back again. Then the teacher said :" Open your eyes children" and in front of the door were two puddles. But beside the second puddle was the inscription: "the Phantom strikes again ! "

At the table I was introduced to Arthur Lismer, a re-

nowned artist, who was one of the famous Canadian Group
of Impressionists called "The Seven". This sensitive white-
haired man had twice visited South Africa to develop child
art centers. At his suggestion I visited him at the Toronto
Art Center behind the City Art Gallery. His "September
Gale" is a renowned Canadian picture. I saw his young art
family being "briefed" round a large rectangular table
where progress on a pageant was being discussed. Each of
the groups of children was to make backgrounds of paper
representing various countries and civilizations, to wear the
appropriate dresses and carry appropriate instruments. Thus
one group of fifteen year olds did classical art, while the
youngest children prepared totems and masks for Red Indian culture, and another group produced Egyptian wigs and
headdresses. Although the community of the Center numbered over five hundred he knew the first names of every
child.

  In his study I saw two paintings by him. One was a
study in red and black depicting intestine-looking forests,
with a central bough which in its projection seemed to pull
the spectator into the forest. The second was a study of
South African natives emphasizing their lithe, sinuous
backs and the brown sheen of their skins; one was longitu-
dinally draped to emphasize the contrast with the vertical
backs of the rest. This doyen of Canadian art was a leg-
pulling, sensitive man who believed that every child had a
potentiality for art, and like all truly great men was modest.
He thought television had great art teaching prospects.
Many years later I would visit the Toronto City Art Gallery
and there see the most complete exhibition of Henry
Moore's sculptures and drawings ever brought together in a
permanent show.

  Having spent so much time at Union Seminary in
New York City, I was looking forwards to visiting the other
major theological center, namely Yale Divinity School, located in New Haven, Connecticut. Its impressive buildings
are in the Georgian Colonial style evoking the university's
origins. Yale University was founded in 1701, its main purpose being a school "wherein youth may be instructed in

the Arts and Sciences who through the blessing of Almighty God may be fitted for Publick Employment both in Church and State." In 1746 a professorship in Divinity was established and this led to a separate Department in 1822 later known as Yale Divinity School. Between 1822 and 1952, 6,955 students had been enrolled, and living graduates in 1952 numbered 2,674 (with B.D., S.T.M., M.A., and Ph.D. degrees) The student body usually included members of thirty to thity-five different Christian bodies and instruction was given in the history, doctrines and polity of all the leading Protestant Churches.

As a church historian I was particularly looking forward to meeting K. S. Latourette and Roland Bainton, both teaching at Yale University Divinity School in New Haven, as well as Robert Calhoun of whom Dr. Van Dusen of Union Seminary had spoken so enthusiastically. I was also to interview the Dean, Dr. Liston Pope.

Latourette was the only member of the Divinity School faculty to be given the honorific title of Sterling Professor, and confessed to me that he was delighted to have been given an Honorary Doctorate of Divinity by Oxford University, an honor shared by Professor Reinhold Niebuhr, and by very few Americans. He won fame for his monumental *History of the Expansion of Christianity* in seven massive volumes This for the first time in English-speaking lands, established the extraordinary impact of Christianity as a missionary religion, and showed that the greatest expansion took place in the world in the nineteeth century, and not in the Middle Ages as some might have surmised. He invited us to breakfast and there we learned that he was of mixed Scotch, Huguenot, Pennsylvania Dutch, and English ancestry and that he had spent several years in China. He was to retire in a year from his "gilt-edged" Sterling Professorship, but would remain at the Divinity Quadrangle. Since he was a Bachelor, he would write his regular quota of words each day and still rejoice in the friendship of the Divinity students who called him "Uncle Ken." His next task would be to write a survey of the foreign policy of the United States for the Institute of

Pacific Studies. He would spend his remaining summers in his house in Oregon. This quiet man had a steady style that calmly made its points and moved on without advertising them.

The other church historian we met was a very dynamic man and he and I found we were both the sons of British Congregational ministers. He has written several books that are exciting reading, but the most widely known is his great biography of Martin Luther, *Here I stand*. which explores to the full the drama and courage in the life of that first and greatest of the sixteenth-century Reformers. One of my treasures is the inscribed copy of the book that he gave me, with characteristic generosity. Typically, it is illustrated with black and white drawings and cartoons, some of which he modified to bring out the point which they were to illustrate. We went into his study and I saw his large collection of visual aids, his Luther pamphlets, and one pamphlet inscribed in Melancthon's handwriting.This man was full of *joie de vivre*. No wonder that with his erudition, visual aids, and jocularity, his classes were widely attended by theological students.

Then I had the privilege of half an hour's walk with Dr. Robert Calhoun, Yale's Professor of Historical Theology, thought by Van Dusen and Bennett to be the most creative theologian in the U.S.A. He had a charitable, brilliant and balanced mind. His *God and the Day's Work* is a superb study of Christian vocation. He said that his next year's Sabbatical leave would be spent in Holland where he would revise for Scribner's his History of Christian Thought lectures. We discussed current trends in theology, and he expressed the view that the world needed the balance of the English-speaking world. He thought Karl Barth was unfair in criticizing American theology, particularly as he had never visited the States despite many invitations, and because he did not appear to know any significant American theological writings. (I agreed with him in this judgment.) He was surprised, he told me, by the sobriety of U.S. military strategists (excepting Generals Patton and MacArthur). He really believed that our military personnel and scientists were developing atomic weapons for field use and not for civilian populations. This was a paradox that the Japanese would not have appreciated. His attitude, however, was characteristically fair, as he was a pacifist by conviction.

I was of two minds about my appointment to interview Dean Liston Pope of Yale Divinity School because he was said to have a "rat-trap mind". However it turned out to be a frank account of the financing of the Yale Divinity School. The budget was approximately $500,000 of which the University provided about one third. The salaries of the faculty seemed generous. Instructors rose from $3,500 per annum by increments of $250 to $4,250 in 3 annual reappointments. An assistant professor's salary began at $4,750 and by three annual additions of $250 reached $5,500, at which time he was either promoted or dropped. A full professor received from $7,500 to $8,500, but a Sterling Professor (a man of special distinction) received some $10,000. Another professor of distinction may also receive a special endowment, as did the Pitkin Professor, R. L. Calhoun. In general, a man may rise from instructor to full professor in 15 years. Assistant Professors and those of the higher ranks could join the university annuity plan by which they contributed 5% of their salary and received an equal percentage from the university. The faculty at that time of Yale Divinity School consisted of 15 full professor,s 5 associate professors, 6 assistant professors, and 4 part-time instructors, a total Faculty of 30 serving a student community of between 350 and 400. This interview was special since usually Americans seemed to me to be secretive on the subject of salaries !

Dean Pope had obviously another human and humorous side. He told my Union Seminary host, Ken Baldwin, this story, which Baldwin repeated to me. Pope said in lecturing to a group of young theologians: "I had to interview a theological student whose academic record was bad, and I ended telling him "Don't worry George, you'll probably have a fine career." Then I added, "But I guess you'd like to spit on my grave." The pan-faced student replied:

'Oh, no, I wouldn't want to do that sir . . . I'd hate to stand in line!'".

The meeting which I had been looking forward to most was that with Professor Reinhold Niebuhr and his wife Dr. Ursula Niebuhr who was Professor of Religion at Barnard College, next door to Union Theological Seminary. This was at supper in their apartment. This tall theological giant of a man I had heard give, without a note, the most rapid and learned ethical address I had ever heard to the spellbound Congregationalists of Britain at their Annual May Meetings in London several years before. He now seemed very tired after a recent operation for thrombosis and, in the circumstances, (coming out of the valley of the shadow but its fogs still clinging) he was a remarkable example of the faith he so finely propounded. In him was commingled brilliance and compassion, and he was a great man and a great Christian, undoubtedly America's most percipient apologist for Christianity. His English wife, Ursula, was cheering him by the device of saying in effect: "It might have been much worse—you haven't completed Job's catalogue yet!"

He said, in reference to the South African situation: "The Germans and the Anglo-Saxons are the worst racists in the world." That made us equal, considering his German and my English background. We discussed the Danish theologian Søren Kierkegaard, or rather, I gave the great man his lead and then listened. He thought him remarkable as aesthete, philosopher and theologian, but he observed: "S.K. mistook passionate subjectivity for faith." He also commented on the difference between Presbyterian and Methodist ethics, observing: "Methodist stewardship is preferable to Presbyterian ethics based on 'The Lord hath prospered me'." I have always admired his correlation of theology and politics and his realism. This was perhaps best expressed in his apothegm: "Man's capacity for justice makes democracy possible; but man's inclination to injustice makes democracy necessary."

This was the high water mark of my visit to North America and was happy that Brenda was there to help in communicating my admiration for his writings. He also told us what his future plans were. They included the preparation of a series of philosophical essays, which he could do by dictaphone and would not involve sustained physical effort. For these I suggested the title "Beyond Sickness." His other project had been suggested to him by his colleague, John Bennett, namely to write a simple exposition of his theology, as Emil Brunner had done in his book, *Our Faith.*

AMERICAN STAR LECTURERS

It was also stimulating to hear the lectures of some of the American theological stars. The most dramatic lecturer in any field that I have ever heard was professor James Muilenburg at Union Theological Seminary in New York City. The lecture was presented in Union's largest lecture room which was crowded. He was rounding off his consideration of Elijah and some interesting points he made in passing were: we would call the juniper tree broom, and that Elijah went into the Negeb to the very cave where Moses received the theophany and therefore expectantly wondering whether the rolling of the earth was the divine voice, or the blistering whirlwind, and then he really heard it "in a thin slice of silence." (I reflected that you can only hear silence when you leave New York City.) God's advice, said Muilenburg, was not vague but embarrassingly precise and simple: "Go to Ahab." He observed with a sneer that "Jezebel was a member of the mercantile class of Phoenicia and had their approach." He modernized her to make her relevant, picturing her "floating" with her pencilled eyebrows towards Ahab and stimulating his dormant egotism.

As I thought over the technique of this lecture that held his audience rivetted for an hour, it seemed to me that he was born a dynamic teacher, who knew the appeal of the heroic, the sardonic, and the unexpected to lively young men and women. As a result, he left behind his notes and addressed the class eye-to-eye directly. He even perambulated about the wide platform and right down the central aisle. He was also a scholar and a man of God. I had never heard such a commanding lecture from members of the faculties of divinity in Edinburgh or Oxford. One very small defect of this type of lecturing, possibly a necessary consequence of it, was that very occasionally he deviated from the theme, but his ability to recover its central thread was very rapid.

A very different kind of lecture by a famous man that I attended at Union Seminary was presented by Professor Paul Tillich, whose discipline was philosophical theology. His students, of whom there must have been about 80 in the classroom, each had concentrated systematic statements or summaries of the lecture in their hands, and he proceeded to read the typescript in his hands slowly and relentlessly. He was a courteous, profound, dignified and clear lecturer . He was comparing the historical and non-historical religions of the world as a preliminary to expounding the uniquely Christian philosophy. This, he said, combined the universal idea of Saviorhood with the particulaized historical sense of destiny. He claimed, and this was an entirely new insight to me, that the doctrine of the Trinity arose from the tension between the universal cosmic and the historical particular resolved in terms of a mediator. I wondered how many of his students fully understood him. I found my own attention wandering because of the immense difficulty of maintaining concentrated attention on dominantly abstract concepts. But I realized I had been listening to a masterly thinker.

During my visit to Drew University in Madison, New Jersey, I was able to contrast the lecturing styles of two outstanding teachers, the one British, and the other American. The British scholar was John Selden Whale, who as Principal of Chestnut College, Cambridge, had given a renowned series of lectures on Christian doctrine that were widely disseminated in book form. The American scholar was Dr. Stanley Romaine Hopper, an expert in the correlation of Theology and Literature.

Dr. Whale's theme was the Atonement, one in a series on the Work of Christ, and his emphasis in this lecture was the reconciliation of the holiness and the love of God in the Cross of Christ. Dr. Hopper's theme was the main emphases of the thought of Rainer Maria Rilke and a Christian critique of these tenets. The difference between their techniques was striking. Dr. Hopper sat in his chair, while Dr. Whale stood, perambulated, and gesticulated. Dr. Hopper encouraged discussion, whereas Dr. Whale preferred that any questions should be put to him privately after the uninterrupted lecture. Dr. Whale gave an admirably phrased lecture, holding the interest of his audience, but his copious illustrations included citations in French, German, Latin and Greek in the original languages. Whale's lecture was an example of brilliant showmanship, but Hopper's was an example of thoughtful modesty. But neither expressed what I found the most striking character of American lecturing, the frequency with which lectures were given extemporaneously, without a note.

FIVE CHURCHES

Five churches were of particular interest to me in this visit to America and I will end with their description. Two of them were university chapels, two others were famous city churches, and the last a genuinely interracial church just starting in Harlem, the Black community in Manhattan.

On Palm Sunday I was present at the lovely neo-Gothic Duke University Chapel, with blue clerestory windows rich in medieval symbolism, with a well-trained choir of 300 undergraduates. Typically there were only two hymns for the congregation to sing, but both were entirely appropriate. The chapel was filled. The service was conducted by Dr. James Cannon, Dean of Duke Divinity School, and the sermon was preached by Dr. Waldo Beach, professor of Social Ethics in the Divinity School, a most genial host to me. The title of the sermon was "The Irony of Triumph" and its major thrust was the explanation that Christ came as the religious Messiah but the people thought he would be a political liberator. The sermon was thoughtful, taut, logical and had several thrusts, including the statement "Jesus was too brash in throwing out the money-changers from the Temple; he ought, we think, to have referred the matter to the Economics Committee of the Temple for reference to a Subcommittee and postponement." It was marked by human touches. For example, after mentioning that Jesus tickled the curiosity of the crowd, he added: "The Sunday School children will be tickling one another's ears with palm branches today." This sermon was, and this is its importance, a vivid account of how easily the purpose of Christ can be misunderstood and misinterpreted.

The second university chapel service I attended was on Easter Sunday at Fisk University in Nashville, Tennessee, where I had been invited to preach by Dean William Faulkner, a great Christian soul who happened to be a dynamic recorder of folktales. The singing by the Jubilee Choir was superb. They had the deep-timbre voices the world associates with Negro Spirituals. The congregation included Blacks, Whites, Japanese, Chinese and Indians—a genuine interracial fellowship. Dean Faulkner took the devotional parts of the service with great dignity and sincerity and in my sermon I was granted great freedom in expressing both the condemnation and the comfort of the Christian Gospel and the Resurrection.

When I visited Fisk's International Center, I had the privilege of meeting a distinguished Black artist, Aaron Douglas, whose fine murals in the Library had attracted me. I was privileged to pick from his portfolio and I chose a delightful pastel, "William" produced in 1950. It depicts a young negro boy in a green hat whose face shows anxiety about the future. This I hung in my study when I returned to South Africa—a living proof of the skill of the artist and the anxiety that Blacks feel when dominated by racist whites. It is now in the living-room of the historian who is my successor at Princeton University as Henry W. Putnam Professor of Religion, Dr. Albert Raboteau, appointed in 1992 Dean of Princeton Graduate School. Such a treasure should indeed belong to an African American.

I also worshipped at two major metropolitan churches, one in Boston, known as The Old South Church, a Congregationalist historic shrine, and at Madison Avenue Presbyterian Church in New York City. The Old South Church has an imposing front in Copley Square, and was founded in 1669. It has a huge auditorium, with stained-glass windows on all sides, a tucked away choir hidden from view in a gallery above and behind the congregation, a Communion-table lacking a cross but with a great display of lilies and a dominating central pulpit. The choral music was superb, including the works of Brahms and C.P.E. Bach, but the congregation (as was often the case in large churches) had only two hymns to sing. The only responsive part of the service was a lection to be found at the back of the hymnal, while the pastoral prayer's responses were sung by the choir alone.

The church was packed. The preacher was an inaptly named senior minister, Dr. Frederick M. Meek, a man with a leonine face and a voice speaking with the power and rapidity of a sten gun. His sermon title was: "Face the attacks on the Faith" and the text which served as its foundation was St. Luke 18:9: "Certain which trusted in themselves that they were righteous." Dr. Meek had a strong face and an even stronger voice. He gave the impression of having rethought his theology confessing that liberal theology had underestimated the deceitfulness of the human heart. He argued the need for a theological offensive because we had not been convinced enough Christians, with the result that Communism, "the mightiest mass movement in evangelism," had made inroads on the world. But what appeared to be missing was an account of the essential doctrines of Christianity and how it should be propagated, apart from enthusiasm. It was admirably illustrated with literary citations from Charlotte Bronte and other authors.

The high point of the service seemed to be the Offertory Procession, introduced by a lengthy announcement, ending with "as the Lord hath prospered you, give of your substance." The substance consisted chiefly of silver half-dollars collected on large round plates by the elegantly

dressed ushers with white carnations in their lapels, who
marched in military step to the Communion table, where
the assistant minister received them, then raised his hands
aloft, followed by a Doxology sung by all. This, I noted,
was the single processional in the service.

Madison Avenue Presbyterian Church in Manhattan
reminded me in two ways of Boston's Old South Church,
because beside its crossless Communion-table there were
two huge bronze vases each filled with a profusion of arum
lilies, and the ushers wore morning coats and striped trou-
sers and white carnations in their button-holes. The choir,
about forty in number, wore gowns while the women also
had juliet-caps. The last to enter were the four ministers
who stood beside the Communion-table, like four well-
groomed undertakers. Each of them had a small part in the
service, except the returning hero, the senior minister, Dr.
George Buttrick, who had just come back from a world tour
of Presbyterian missions, and this would be the topic of his
address. He seemed to me a mixture of Amos the prophet
and Harry Truman the President, speaking in the Northern
accents of English Blackpool. His curious windmill gestures and apparently artificial smile were disadvantages, but
his seriousness no one could doubt, nor his central Christian convictions. Here was a genuine man of faith. He was
a penetrating analyst of his experiences round the world.
He described himself as "much sobered" by the 5,000 mile
trip made under the auspices of the Board of Foreign Missions of the Presbyterian Church of America. He had delivered 250 sermons and speeches and homilies in more than
20 countries and in 3 continents, so it was reported in next
day's *New York Herald Tribune*. These facts were not mentioned in his address.

Dr. Buttrick had obviously been shaken by his recent experiences. He stated that the world situation was
"hopeless if our hope would lie in man." He insisted that armaments were not enough of themselves to defeat or keep
away Communism. He said: "Perhaps Stalin is glad to see
us pouring our substance into armaments. I do not know. At
any rate, he is hardly such a fool as to go into atomic war

while all Asia may yet fall into his hands like a ripe plum."
His central thesis was phrased thus: "Russia talks peace and
means war: the United States talks war and means peace,
and the oppressed nations take us at our word!" These were
hard words for a plutocratic congregation to hear and Dr.
Buttrick did not pull his punches. Throughout the implication was that Christianity must empower its mission stations with convinced and dedicated missionaries, generously supported by the Churches.

On another Sunday I heard Dr. Buttrick preach a
more formal sermon on the changelessness of God in a
transitory world (in which the very conception of God was
changing). But even here he attacked the conservative type
of human whose escutcheon he wittily claimed was "For
weal or woe, my status is always quo." He was editor-in-
chief of the projected eight-volume "Interpreters Bible"
(volumes 7 and 8 had already appeared) which combine the
interpretations of each Biblical passage by a scholar and its
application by a preacher.

If one felt the Biblical presence of Dives in the
well-heeled congregation, one could see many companions
of Lazarus in the East Harlem Church I am about to describe in its beginnings in a poor suburb of New York City.
I was taken to see the work of the newly formed Protestant
Parish by Dr. George Webber, then Dean of men students
at Union Theological Seminary and now President of New
York Theological Seminary. As he drove he explained that
the area of East Harlem was populated chiefly by poor
Blacks and Puerto Ricans, and that he and his helpers were
starting from the ground up. They had taken over a basement which cost them $50.00 per month, and in it they had
installed a harmonium, folding chairs, a table, a cross, an
open Bible, and two candlesticks—the last three items
standing on the table. This was all the furnishing of the
simply named "Church of the Redeemer".

I was present with about eight other persons at a
leaders' dedication service. Here I was able to sense the
deep desire to help the unfortunate, with the conviction that
social service alone was no substitute for the Christian

faith, and that here they were combining the preaching of a transhistorical faith with occasional acts of social witness. As an example of the latter, I was told how the whole of the residents in a certain neighborhood emphasized the filthiness of their living conditions by a public sweep of the streets as a protest. I was fascinated when Dean Webber showed me a vacant filth-strewn area between two blocks of tenements. Here he and his helpers had put on a play dealing with the social and religious interests of the neighborhood and were watched by hundreds upon hundreds, leaning out of their windows.

In the three years in which Webber and Company had been operating, they had established three area centers. The following approximate figures testify to their success in the midst of many difficulties in the three centers they had. In the first they had 60 adults, 75 Sunday scholars, and about 100 teenagers; in the second center they gained 35 adults, 60 Sunday scholars, and 75 teenagers. In the third center they had about 10 adults, 20 Sunday scholars, and 25 teenagers. In the course of my visit Dean Webber made two very relevant remarks. One was that this society of shiftless persons was matriarchal, for fathers come and go. The other was that "a pie-in-the-sky when you die" theology still had considerable relevance and helpfulness in a situation where there was little likelihood of a change in the social environment, as long as it did not deaden responsibility on the part of the more privileged Christians. How I admired this man and his helpers!

6

TEACHING AT OXFORD UNIVERSITY
1953-1955

After my visit to North America I returned for half a year to Rhodes University. My academic time was packed with attempts to improve the Department of Divinity. It was also a heavily interrupted time, because most weekends were spent visiting the Congregational Churches as Chairman of the Congregational Union of South Africa. I was greatly impressed by the strong corporate sense of community in the Black churches and the welcome that I received among them as a Caucasian. In the churches they found an understanding and a compassion that was refused them in national life.

My other major interruption at this time was spent in the serious consideration of a pressing invitation to return to Oxford as Senior Lecturer in Ecclesiastical History in Mansfield and Regent's Park Colleges, two theological colleges that were recognized as providing part of the lecturing strength in Oxford University's Faculty of Divinity. As I will indicate later, it was a difficult decision whether to accept or to turn down this invitation.

The final days at Rhodes University were saddened by the prospect of leaving my theological students grateful for what I had tried to do and my colleagues in the Department and beyond. I was, however cheered by several considerations. Two of the brighter students, MacGregor and Woolf, provided written testimonies of their appreciation. My earliest academic collaborator, Leslie Hewson, as Warden of Livingstone House, arranged a farewell party for my

wife and myself which my mother-in-law, Mrs. Ethel Deakin—an English lady of the greatest dignity combined with
warmth—attended. We were presented with a beautiful im-
buia table, a series of books and a host of good wishes.

I will cite the satirical but jocular verse of Archie
MacGregor because it refers to some of my oddities. It was
titled: "The Lay of the Last Lecture."

> Weep, all ye theologians,
>   And let your hearts be riven:
> Our prof's about to leave us,
>   But not (as yet), for heaven. . .
>
> No longer shall we hear him,
>   In lectures theological,
> Expounding doctrines teleo-
>   Cosmo- and also onto-logical.
>
> No more we'll join, in classes,
>   In controversial binge,
> Where he contributes opinions,
>   With an ecumenic tinge.
>
> No more we'll hear his footfall,
>   Rather late, upon the stairs,
> See his smile, apologetic,
>   That precedes his breathless prayers.
>
> Nor further shall we see him
>   Bravely vaunting in the breeze,
> Those vari-coloured neckties
>   That would e'en Picasso please.
>
> BUT HE'S LEFT US NOW FOR ISIS,
>   AND THE QUADS AND HALLS OF OXON.,
> TO PRECIPITATE A CRISIS
>   WITH HIS MULTI-COLOURED SOX-ON!

John Woolf provided an article full of appreciation in *The Livingstonian*—the house organ of the Theological Hostel at Rhodes—which is embarrassingly flattering, from which a few paragraphs only will be quoted. Of my lectures he wrote:

> He combines with a beautiful speaking voice, great beauty of expression . . . a rich vocabulary and attractive imagery. . . . When Dr. Davies has the characteristic twinkle in his eye, then he is sure to be on the point of telling some witty story, or of using some startling up-to-date phrase to describe some point in his lecture.

He also claims:

> . . .While among his students, he is a man among men. He commands their admiration and respect, and possesses the rare gift of making students feel that they are capable of discussing matters with him on his own high intellectual level, which has the effect of creating a lasting desire to deserve the honour.

The article continues with a description of some of my peculiarities.

> If there is anything he dislikes, then it is pomposity, particularly in parsons . . . he is the champion of the underdog. Students past and present will take comfort in the knowledge that Dr. Davies dislikes the traditional things that are good for one, e.g. a balanced diet, invigorating exercise, hard, upright chairs, etc. A frequent dictum is: "The hardest step in the life of a Christian man is from the bed to the floor in the morning." Ecclesiastical dislikes include a peculiar abhorrence of children's addresses, women knitting at meetings (whom he terms "knit-wits") and the beating of the denominational drum.

And later on my love of travel, he adds:

> He shows a marked preference for getting to his des-
> tination as speedily as possible, as anyone who has
> been a passenger in his car will rather shakenly con-
> firm. Connected possibly with his admiration for both
> medieval and post-impressionist art is the fact that he
> likes *violent colors.*

In commenting on my convictions, John Woolf
mentioned my ecumenism, my color-blindness in racial
matters as a deep Christian conviction that all are made in
the image of God, and my desire that all the great historic
liturgies of Christendom should be appreciated. He empha-
sizes the latter point by a citation from my very first book
to be published, *Christian Worship: Its Making and Meaning* (1946). This view I still adhere to as an historian, although I recognize the need for new forms of worship. This
citation goes as follows:

> Ancient cathedrals or parish churches remind the
> worshippers that "other men have laboured and ye
> have entered into their labours", that the Christian
> Church has weathered many storms and that "the
> gates of hell shall not prevail against it." Further-
> more, they serve as a perpetual reminder of the Com-
> munion of Saints. The chief advantage of a Christian
> edifice is that it preaches to the eye, as sermons
> preach to the ear.

Even when preparing to leave South Africa, I was
still of two minds about the decision. The one College,
Mansfield, was familiar to me as an alumnus, and the other,
Regent's Park College, a Baptist foundation, had been
transferred from London (hence the title) to Oxford and enjoyed an excellent reputation. In some ways, I was exceedingly reluctant to leave South Africa, but the prestige of
Oxford and its great research facilities in the Bodleian Library, my wife's eagerness to return to her homeland and

her anxiety about the health of our son, Hugh, all made me accept the invitation.

The most serious drawback was that the salary (apart from a rent-free house) was exactly a quarter of what I had been receiving at Rhodes University. To make both ends meet I had to add to my income by accepting invitations to preach in small rural churches in Oxfordshire for a pittance. Teaching bright Oxonians was, however, a great consolation, though the climate in sunny South Africa was much preferable to the clouded, rainy and misty days in England.

What had chiefly attracted me to return to Oxford was the warmth of the invitation which was conveyed by Dr. Will Moore, Chairman of the Board of Governors of Mansfield College, and himself a Fellow of St. John's College, who had visited me in Grahamstown while on a tour of stations of the London Missionary Society. I was persuaded that under the leadership of the new Principal of Mansfield, Dr. John Marsh, Chaplain of the College when I was studying for my doctorate there, the College would strive to retain its theological emphasis but also aim to become a full multi-disciplinary College of Oxford University. In recent years, building on the Marsh, Caird and Sykes heritage, it has been assured that provided it can raise the necessary funds, it will attain its hope.

On the return voyage to England I was greatly cheered by three companions. One, Father Fontaine, a Roman Catholic missionary in Nyasaland, was leaving his community for a glimpse of home in Quebec Province. We discussed the prospects for missions.

The second person with whom we consorted was Canon Edward Patterson, an Anglican artist-missionary whom I had met before in his renowned center near Bulawayo, at Cyrene, where he had spent sixteen years. He and his wife were going to spend the best part of a year combining deputation work at week-ends with weekdays at London's Central School of Arts and Crafts. His colorful personality matched his aesthetic ability, because he won the first men's prize in the Fancy Dress Competition aboard as a Spanish organ-grinder complete with a realistic monkey. You could count on his success in exhibiting the paintings and carvings of his Southern Rhodesian African boys.

The third member of our clerical group was the young South African Methodist minister, Victor J. Bredenkamp, and one of my former outstanding students. He and his wife Marie, were determined to save and borrow enough to come to Oxford University, and I was delighted to think that he would be a member of my old College and the one in which I was to lecture, Mansfield. His first experience with an Oxford landlady turned out to be unusual. They had to compete for their breakfast with a jackdaw, which took an indecent interest in their Marmite and left tell-tale streaks on the table-cloth. Their next flat, to their joy, lacked an aviary. He is now Professor and Head of the Department of Divinity at Natal University in Pietermaritzburg. In his own personality and intensity of study, this highly competent young man represented a line of continuity between my work in Rhodes and Oxford Universities, and even came to Princeton University to gain a Ph.D. in Old Testament studies. And the boat trip proved the possibility of joyful trans-denominational ecumenical fellowship.

My number of lecturing hours at Oxford were fewer each week and the terms were shorter than had been the case in South Africa, but since I was responsible for tutorials in two institutions I had about eighteen hours each week devoted to this highly individual form of instruction. This was exhausting. On the other hand, I gave the lectures on the Reformation to a large University audience, which was immensely stimulating. Furthermore, during the brief summer term, I was able to lecture on any theme I wished, and this gave me the opportunity of trying out my researches into English Church History, which I had not been able to use directly in South Africa because it did not seem relevant there.

It was also interesting to be involved once again in the training of ordinands as preachers in sermon class, a task which I shared with the Principals of the two institutions. We tested the men for the accuracy of their interpretation of Scripture, for the clarity and relevance of the message, for the sequence of the thoughts, and for the vividness of the illustrations, and the practicality of the discourse. One could only hope that this instruction would make sermons both more interesting and more helpful in hundreds of churches in the future.

I also had an institutional task, namely that of helping to combine the teaching of Eccesiastical History in the two Colleges, with the help of a Lecturer in each of them. The Mansfield Lecturer in Church History was Dr. Erik Routley, also the College Organist, and a superbly witty lecturer on any topic, whose fame as a hymnologist was renowned throughout England, as it was later to become throughout the United States. He understandably demurred at my being termed "Senior Lecturer" because he had been longer than I at Mansfield and we were roughly the same age. My Lecturer in Ecclesiastical History at Regent's Park College was Dr. Morris West, an expert in the early history of the Baptists in England and in Europe, and a genial man, several years younger than myself. I think we all fulfilled our task well which included not only lecturing, and tutoring, but also advising both B. Litt. and D. Phil. students. The latter responsibility delighted me, and, in fact, I had more research students to advise than any other Divinity faculty member in the university, so I was informed. In these years I became adept at judging dissertations in British Church History of the modern period, and ecumenical theses. Our department in Grahamstown was too young to have provided doctoral students in my time.

I recall one very amusing incident in which I was coexternal examiner with Professor Norman Sykes of Cambridge University, a brilliant Yorkshireman, in which we disagreed with each other over a Welsh candidate for a D. Phil. I readily agreed that his dissertation was not of doctoral standard, but I wanted the disappointed candidate to be given a consolation B. Litt. degree for his pains. Our discussion was taking place in the Oxford streets in a small Austin convertible I was driving, and as I became excited in the discussion, my fellow examiner began to worry about our safety and, I believe, for that reason, concurred reluctantly with my judgment!

Oxford Senior Common Rooms, which were a new experience for me, proved to be great delights. After unusually high quality dinners, preceded by sherry, accompanied by excellent wines and topped off after the meal with liqueurs, the standard of the conversations, while occasionally scatological, were usually erudite and very often spiced with lively witticisms. I remember three Colleges in which I was invited by one of the Fellows or Professors, which provided particularly memorable experiences. One was at New College, where Mervyn Thomas, (like myself the son of a Welsh Congregational minister), and a University don in French, invited me. After visiting the chapel at New College together, and noting the superb Epstein sculpture of Lazarus and the rather incongruous stained-glass saints painted by Sir Joshua Reynolds, we repaired to the dining hall where the conversation sparkled with anecdotes and wit, and in which Lord David Cecil, University Professor of English Literature, contributed to the liveliness. On another occasion, the University Professor of Ecclesiastical History invited me to Christ Church, Oxford's largest College, and for the only time in my life I dined sumptuously on gold plates. These plates were, I believe, the gift of Cardinal Wolsey, founder of the College. It was also a pleasure for me to be invited to Jesus College, which has close associations with Wales, where the Senior Tutor who invited me was renowned for his almost creative capacity for absent-mindedness and, therefore, shall remain unnamed. Dons from Exeter and Lincoln Colleges, next to each other, also invited me to dine there. All these occasions were enjoyable. Also at Mansfield College once a week the dons dined together and invited friends to share the meal from other Colleges, and Regent's Park did the same, but without the libations that eased conversation.

It was also wonderful to be back in the most ecumenical College Chapel that I know, that of Mansfield College. Here were reproductions of the badges of the great universities of Britain and the United States with the images of the great Christian leaders that had been associated with them, and founders or leaders of denominations like George Fox, John Bunyan and John Wesley, who was represented in a statue. Here appeared the black and orange crest of Princeton University with the image of one of its Presidents, namely the great theologian Jonathan Edwards. Earlier theologians like Origen and Augustine could also be found in the same chapel.

One of the major conveniences of England's location is its close proximity to Continental Europe for vacation visits. One of my great pleasures in what turned out to be only a twenty-seven month stay in England was a stimulating visit to Holland with my wife. For me the hardships endured with courage by the citizens of Rotterdam during World War II are perfectly symbolized by a statue designed by the Russian sculptor Zadkine. In future years this will be the only visible sign of the sufferings endured by the people of this city, an experience paralleled in many other Dutch cities. Its bronze tree stump is a reminder of the trees destroyed in the fire-bombings of May 1940, and the entire statue with its split and upturned human body tells of the desolation, the flames, the trials, the bitterness and the despair of those trying days, but at the same time it speaks of the heroic spirit of the citizens of the desolate city fired by a firm desire to revive and to survive, to triumph over chaos, and to be liberated from the demonic powers that rained destruction upon them.

It was a high point of our visit in the summer of 1954 to see how liberal the race attitudes of the Dutch seemed to be. This was partly, of course, because the racial problem was never as acute in the Netherlands as in South Africa, but even more important was the fact that they had seen at first hand the horrors of racialism in the Nazi treatment of the Jews. In Amsterdam the Nazis had put to death 9,000 Jews, and in Rotterdam there were 8,000 Jews murdered. I was shown near the Central Station in Amsterdam the place where two Germans revisiting the scenes of their crimes had said a few months before, "I see we haven't

killed all the devils off." I was told that immediately four
Dutchmen, all non-Jews, threw the insolent German and his
friend from his car out onto the street. I also learned that
when crowds of Germans visited the tulip fields in the
Spring, many café-notices carried the legend: "Not for Germans." In Leiden I noticed Indonesian students of dark hue
sitting unselfconsciously with Dutch student friends, and I
rejoiced. I recalled the stories of how many *predikants* (literally, preachers, but generally ministers) had risked their
lives to shelter Jewish families. I was told how Professor J.
van Holk, who taught philosophy at Leiden University,
when the S.S. men came to remove the Jewish students of
the university to concentration camps, announced and delivered a public lecture, entitled: "Spinoza—the brilliant
Jew." He, too, was taken away to a prison camp.

A significant political development had recently
taken place in Holland. The Dutch sense of social justice
has made the main character of the dominant political party
socialistic. Within it were two important non-Marxist
groups, the one Catholic and the other Protestant. It was the
Protestant group that deplored the recent ban of the Roman
Catholic Archbishop of Utrecht on the Catholic group. The
most thoughtful men I met claimed that the Dutch Labor
Party represented the finest way of meeting Marxism by accepting the principles of social justice as the true consequence of Christian compassion.

My final impression is a vivid assortment of images: canals, windmills, blue and white Delft pottery, the
cheapness of cigars and the puffs of them which punctuated
speeches, Persian rugs decorating walls and tables as well
as floors, the lovely precision of Vermeer's indoor scenes,
the Biblical depth of Rembrandt's etchings, and the riot of
glory that is Van Gogh after he found the sun in Provence,
and the jollity of Franz Hals, and above all, the linguistic
brilliance and the intrepid courage of the Dutch.

The other great personal event of the Oxford years
was the birth of our second son, Philip. Our lesser delight
was a book I wrote, the only really popular one in almost

forty years, under the title of *Christian Deviations*. It became an astounding success in paperback under the Student Christian Movement imprint in England and that of the Westminster Press, Philadelphia imprint in the United States. To my amazement, it went on selling from March 1954 until the fourth revised edition appeared in 1972, with twelve impressions in between. It appeared in Chinese, German, and French translations also, and the total number of copies sold was over 150,000. I attribute its success to its timeliness as a warning against other imitations of Christianity than the mainline Catholic, Orthodox and Protestant Churches, that had diluted or distorted the traditional Christian affirmations in the ecumenical creeds. Its ultimate benefit for our family was that it made it possible for me to put down over half the price of a small cottage in Vermont which we could rent to skiers in winter and live in ourselves in the summer away from the torrid heat and humidity of Princeton in July and August.

It was most fortunate that I was in England to celebrate with the entire Davies family my father's seventieth birthday in a small village near Southampton to which he had retired when his health weakened. It was a most joyful occasion and we pulled his leg mercilessly. For that purpose I had collected reminiscences of him from different members of the family, and I put it into doggerel. I hope extensive extracts will amuse the reader.

INTRODUCTION

From Guildford and from Redhill, and from Milford-on-the-sea
    From Caterham and Oxford, comes the Davies family.
To celebrate this March, in nineteen-fifty-five
    The fact that Dad is seventy and very much alive!
Husband and father, uncle and grandpa as well:
    Preacher, Poulterer and Poet; and a Stoker fit for Hell!

A driver of great daring, who doesn't know how to stop;
   He accelerates through obstacles, and curses every cop!

A Man of fortitude and spirit (though cider is his drink)
   He overthrows the ladies with the cunning of his wink.
A golfer in his prime, and a singer of strange tunes,
   Who stuffed his wooden canteen full of golfing silver spoons.

You've missed a great experience, if you've never heard him sigh,
   "For a son of the desert am I."
A King of the Desert has big ideas, of course;
   He once built a cat-house of a size to fit a horse!

But it's the largeness of his heart we would celebrate tonight.
   The warmth of his affection, his devotion to the Right,
And half of the achievement of his altruistic life
   Is due to the companionship of his devoted wife.

I now propose to tell, and you shall share the glory,
   In accents appropriate, the MARLAIS DAVIES
      STORY. . .

                    THE POWERFUL PREACHER

Hear the roll-call of the churches this preacher then took on
   Llandilo and Blaenogwy, and Mount Zion, Newport, Mon.
He was gentle to the erring, sympathetic to the sad;
   He was poison to the hypocrite, and strychnine to the cad:
And they made him bang the pulpit as if he'd gone stark staring mad!

Beneath him in the Big Seat the deacons cowered in despair
   As they dodged his irate spittle that came sprinkling through the air.
He sang at all their socials; he was a bard at competitions,
   And his sermons were reported in all the last editions.
The deacons were delighted by his expositions of the Scriptures,
   Yet wounded in their consciences by all his pointed strictures;
Farewell presentations were interrupted by their grief;
   But now that he was going they accepted with relief.

For the knowledge of their secrets, like a dustman's lore of bins
Was embarrassingly personal; he was an expert on their sins!

While a minister at Newport, he attended Cardiff Univ. College;
    And in the Economics class he grabbed thruppenny bits of knowl-
        edge.
But it was on the sports field that he blazed the Davies name;
    A high jump of six-foot two is father's lasting claim to fame!
What was it gave the impetus, and stretched his sinews to the full?
    I'll let you know in secret—his tutor was a bull!

But the finest church he had, the best the sun shone on,
    Was the miners' Christian citadel, in Capel Seion, Cwmavon.
The Liberal-minded deacons put their hands upon their ears,
    For a "Bolshie" in the pulpit confirmed their hidden fears;
"O, we know the man is eloquent," the worried deacons said,
    "We'd forgive his sins being scarlet if his politics weren't red!"

If he'd yielded to the miners, they'd have made him an M.P.
So, salute the mem'ry of *Lord* Marlais, Chairman of the T.U.C.*

*An abbreviation for the Trades Union Congress

THE LANCASHIRE LAD AND
GREENOCK'S GODSEND

So famous was his preaching, so wide his reputation,
    That there came to Wales to hear him a Mancunian deputation
Which claimed him as an orator, and in a double sense,
    Selected him as minister of glorious "Providence".
So his language changed from "T--d--" to a softly uttered "Damn"
    As his diet switched from bread and cheese to potato-pies and ham...
There were shadows in those days, of unemployment and of strife
    That found reflections in Dad's book: "The Problems of [my] Life"
When he left the damp of Manchester for Greenock with his darling,
    It seemed as if for them alone the Scottish pipes were skirling.

Dad's schemes grew yet more reckless, was there ever such a fella'?
He grew commercial mushrooms in the dankness of his cellar! . . .

Because his hand was always on the moving pulse of knowledge,
Mister became *Doctor* D.M.D. of Philadelphia College
With a gown of rich black silk and a hood of flaming red,
That showed to great advantage his very handsome head.

But all good things are bound to come to an end,
After seven brief years the Davies clan Southampton-wards did
bend.

THE HERO OF THE BLITZ

His ministry was started in the year of nineteen-thirty-nine
When only Winston Churchill knew the menace massing on the
Rhine.
The fortress burgh of Henry the Fifth awoke in the dead of night,
As the fire-bombs fell, like flames from Hell, and set the town alight.
Many craven cowards fled, but the anxious brave just stayed,
And took new heart from their minister who never was dismayed.

Through unexploded bombs, and bursting mains, he forced his way to
the docks
To cheer the men of the little ships, who took the hardest knocks.

His heart filled with pride,
Like the ever-swelling tide,
As he pondered on his son,
The gallant Merchant man.
Each time the boy came sailing home, his ship had grown much smaller
But the rings on his arm were greater, and his stories they grew taller!

Till the day arrived when the fighting ceased, and the final shot was
fired,
And Dorian became Rear-Admiral (E) of a rowing-boat (Retired!)
The family is proud of Dad for facing one more fight

Against the threat of loss of sight, in the ever-deepening night.
In torments acute, both anguished and mute, he stuck to his faith in the
 right
And the God in Whom is no darkness, restored the gift of sight.

SEVENTY ONWARDS!

. . . Now when life is growing slothful for the man who has no hope,
We see the family guardian peering through the future's telescope;
 Like the visionary on Patmos, his face in wreathed in smiles,
 John saw the Islands of the Blest, but Dad the Channel Isles!

So Dad and Mum, we toast you both, and bless you for your care!
 And ask that for the latest voyage the weather may be fair!

To our great joy, Father lived another eleven years as minister in the island of Jersey, where we visited him from England and later from the United States.

Ironically for me, the most exciting day in my professional life at Oxford was when I received a letter from Professor George F. Thomas, inquiring if I would be interested in being interviewed for a post as Professor of Religion in the new Department at Princeton University of which he was the founder as well as the Professor of Philosophy of Religion. I was profoundly interested and went for the interview in Princeton during the weekend of April 18th, 1952 and was there when the most famous citizen of Princeton died, Dr. Albert Einstein.

TEACHING AT PRINCETON UNIVERSITY:
EARLY YEARS

Traveling overnight by air from London to New York, I was met by Mrs. George Thomas at a very early hour and was driven to Princeton for the most hectic and penetrating series of academic interviews I have ever experienced. It began immediately after breakfast in the Thomas home, when it appeared that three members of the Department on Religion would put me through my paces. In preparation the theological ethicist, Paul Ramsey, renowned for his *Basic Christian Ethics*, had read my *The Worship of the English Puritans* and both Professor George Thomas and Associate Professor Philip H. Ashby, who taught Comparative Religion, and was a Methodist, had conned my shorter volume, *The English Free Churches*. I assume that they approved of them in general or I would not have been invited for the interview. Both were, however, books which would have been appropriate for a Free Church theological professor, and I think the real interest of my questioners is how well I would fit in to the new program at graduate and undergraduate level which would be aimed, not at the training of ministers, but at showing the relevance of religion to social and cultural life for future teachers in universities. The intense questioning, which while always courteous, was also always direct and continued throughout the morning with a break for lunch. This carried on through the afternoon, with a break for dinner. In the evening the questioning was led by professors of allied departments. For example, a highly regarded professor of the History Department,

Dr. E. Harris Harbison, questioned me about the Reformation, appropriately since his major writing was in that area,
and because I had taught the Reformation in public lectures
at Oxford. Present also was the Dean of Faculty, a kindly
economist, but one used to sizing up the inadequacy of university teachers. After a long, tiring day, I was glad to
sleep.

The next morning, which was a Saturday, I was to
meet the President of the University, Dr. Harold Dodds in
his Italianate mansion in the center of the University surrounded by flowering gardens. He joked that he was always
being confused with Professor C. H. Dodd, the New Testament scholar of Cambridge University. This gave me the
chance to repeat the limerick about Dodd:

> There is a young fellow named Dodd,
> Whose behavior's remarkably odd;
> He spells, if you please,
> His name with three Ds,
> When one is sufficient for God!

Then we continued to talk pleasantly and light-
heartedly. I felt here was a man I could always consult with
confidence, which was exactly the impact made upon me
by Professor George Thomas, a former Rhodes Scholar
with a fine mind and a decent and generous spirit.

The next morning I attended the vast and elegant
Neo-Gothic University Chapel and as we left the service, I
was introduced to a young clergyman who said to me, "My
uncle tells me you are coming to teach in the new program
in Princeton." I merely nodded, not knowing whether I was
or wasn't. But a short time afterwards I asked Professor
Thomas who was the uncle of the young clergyman to
whom he had introduced me, and he replied, "President
Dodds." Thus, quite indirectly, I assumed that I had satisfied my examiners, although I would not know for sure until I received a warm letter from Dr. Thomas with the invitation.

Two difficulties stood in the way of my coming to Princeton in the autumn semester of 1955. The first was that I had to give advance notice to Principal Marsh that I would be leaving at the end of the Oxford Christmas term, and he received the news courteously. The second snag would appear in the autumn when a pulmonary specialist at the Oxford Hospital reported that my lungs were not in the best condition, but told me not to worry unduly about my smoking habits because he had not given up smoking. Although well-intended, this was very bad advice as I would learn some years later. This report, however, was given to the American Embassy and resulted in the unwillingness of its officials to give me an entry permit into the United States. To my surprise this was countermanded by the American Secretary of State, Foster Dulles, a Princeton graduate who was approached urgently on my behalf by President Dodds. And the same gentleman, Dr. Dodds, wrote me a letter in which he said the University would be willing for me to postpone my appointment for a year and defray the cost of my getting treatment in a Swiss sanitarium. I declined the offer, but was deeply impressed by its generosity.

During my rushed visit to Princeton I had learned that the two other additions to the faculty of the Department of Religion were noted scholars in Old and New Testament Studies. Professor R. B. Y. Scott, whom I had met three years before at McGill University in Montreal was the author of a widely read book, *The Relevance of the Prophets,* and also of *The Psalms as Christian Praise*, as well as of Biblical commentaries in important series. He had been awarded three honorary doctorates, two in Canada and the D. D. of Aberdeen University. He and I played golf together, marked in both cases by enthusiasm rather than accuracy. In fact Bob Scott invented what I called the "archaeological stroke" in which his driver dug into the ground, threw up soil, and managed to bury his ball! My golf strokes were much less ingenious.

The other new colleague was a Welshman, W.D. Davies, a pupil of C. H. Dodd, who had written the immensely erudite, *St. Paul and Rabbinic Judaism*, which showed a command of Greek (both classical and Hellenistic), Hebrew, and the tongue that Jesus used, Aramaic. Davies was also a celebrated absent-minded man. On one occasion he was talking to a student on the Duke University campus when he asked him from what direction he (Davies) had come. On learning that he had come from the direction of the dining facility, he observed, "Good, then I don't need to go back there for a meal."

In January of 1956 we crossed the Atlantic with Brenda, my wife, Christine, Hugh, and young Philip, our three children. The transition to America was made easier for the parents by the experience of the previous visit to the U.S.A. It was also eased by the extraordinary generosity of Dorothy Thomas, who became a lifetime friend, who insisted that we take over her house for the first fortnight, while she and her husband went into a hotel. It was the same spirit which delighted in entertaining the faculty frequently in her home for dinner, and who invited both faculty and graduate students each Christmas for a repast and carols in their home. Then we moved to a pleasant apartment in Prospect Street which is almost entirely an extension of the university, since it houses the fraternity clubhouses, the Woodrow Wilson School of Politics (named for the man who was President of the University before becoming President of the United States), and several faculty residences. It would have been possible for me conveniently to walk to the University, but I am addicted to automobiles and I was glad to be able to buy a secondhand Buick, admittedly a little loud in its triple colors.

The two older children settled happily into the local schools, and would use them until my first leave in 1960, when we returned to England and Christine attended the Perse School for Girls and Hugh the Perse School, which he liked so much that although he was only just eight, he wished to stay on there in Cambridge as a boarder going to my family for the vacations. Christine gained high marks in her examinations at school, but since 70% by English custom is a high grade, this was not credited at all on our return to Princeton so that we had to transfer her from Princeton High School to Miss Fine's School, a private School in Princeton, to be sure that she would continue in the College stream. When Hugh finally returned from England, he went to a famous New England Boarding School, Groton School in Massachusetts, where President Franklin Delano Roosevelt had been a student. We would not have dreamed of sending him there had not the Revd. John Crocker, Headmaster of Groton, and the Chairman of the Advisory Board of the University Department of Religion, offered a place to any departmental faculty member's child who could get in. Thus Hugh had an unusually good academic training with a generous scholarship. One of his schoolmates also from Princeton was the son of the distinguished diplomat, George F. Kennan. Ultimately Hugh gained admission to Princeton where he distinguished himself, and Christine gained admission to Smith College, Northampton, where she graduated with a good major in Religion—to my delight. Philip went to the George School, a Quaker day and boarding school, just one hour's car ride away, and from there to Bard College for just three semesters, but his superb photography portfolio some years later gained him a six years scholarship to the federally supported College of Art, namely, that of Boston, where he was intensely happy. Hugh gained his Princeton A. B. *summa cum laude* in the Department of Art and Archeology, and then went on to gain his M.F.A. and Ph. D. also at Princeton University. It was a great delight for his mother and I that, after his absence in England and distance from us at Groton, we saw so much of him during the nine years he was at Princeton.

My first year of teaching at Princeton was comparatively easy. I was first introduced to a Princeton University teaching concept I had not met before. It was called a "precept." Each course which was taught by public lectures, two or three a week, was then sub-divided into groups of eight students in those days, and each of them had a preceptor whose responsibility it was to provoke them into discussion and the clarification of the ideas in the prescribed reading for that week. While it did not give the student a one-to-one correlation with the instructor as at Oxford, it was an admirable compromise. During the Spring semester I listened with great appreciation to the lectures on the Philosophy of Religion delivered without a note by Professor Thomas. They were marked by analytical depth, clarity, and the greatest fairness in expounding theories which he did not himself agree with, and they conveyed a great respect for both faith and human intelligence. Being used to the relative shyness of the Oxford undergraduates, I was surprised by the boldness and freedom with which the Princeton undergraduates criticized both lecturer and readings, but many criticisms were thoughtful. The shyer persons had little opportunity to contribute to the discussion, so that I made a point of inviting them to speak, out of fairness, in trying to silence the repetitive loud-mouths.

My other responsibility was to direct a Graduate Seminar in the History of Christianity for our Ph. D. students, who were required to take three seminars a semester for four semesters, two of the twelve had to be in an allied Department beyond Religion and when all twelve had been completed satisfactorily, they took a set of examinations termed "The Generals". If they passed these they gained the M.A. degree and then immediately planned and wrote their doctoral dissertations.

I was also used as an advisor for the A. B. students majoring in the Department who were all required to write a Senior Thesis, a fine innovation introduced by Princeton to encourage clear writing of English, the use of the imagination, and the experience of creativity. This was done at a level that amazed me and it was to become one of my annual delights to take my share in advising the writers of "Senior Theses." I shall on a later occasion give some examples of the most original or profound or creative theses that were prepared by final year undergraduates.

When summer approached, the Thomases who knew their England well and its temperate climate, and imagined how intolerable we would find the steaming days of Princeton, advised me to write to the Chairman of two or three of the Associations of Congregational Churches in the

New England States, asking if they could refer me to ministers in their area who might let our family have the holiday use of their manse if I conducted the services and preached free of charge. In this way for several summers we lived in parsonages for a month at a time in both Connecticut and Vermont. For two successive years I was interim minister at the lovely Congregational Church in the heart of Connecticut at Brookfield Center near to Lake Candlewood, where a local physician took us out often on his motorboat, and where the congregation included a history professor at Columbia and the Dean of the Faculty at Barnard College for Women, next door to Columbia University, and high-powered business men and women. I did, however, have one daunting week-end at the Brookfield Congregational Church, which, thankfully, was not typical.

I had been lecturing all week at Union Theological Seminary in Manhattan, and was preparing the worship and conning the sermon for the next morning, when about 10. o'clock on a Saturday night the doorbell rang, and a young woman apologized for coming at that hour. She told me that she was the common-law wife of a Trans-World-Airline pilot who had died in the crash of his plane in Italy, and she would like me to arrange a small memorial service for him in Brookfield to which his co-pilots would be invited. Naturally, I agreed and this was done the next afternoon. Then, I had only just finished a lecture at Union Theological Seminary on the following morning, when a deacon of the Brookfield Church informed me that the young son of the Superintendent of the Sunday School had climbed a tree in the orchard and fallen on a live wire and been electrocuted, so would I come back that evening and plan a funeral service for him? I did, but it was exceedingly difficult since I was a newcomer with an unAmerican accent. It is the pastoral familiarity with Christian people built upon regular visitation and knowledge of families that begets the warmth of affection that helps people in time of crisis. As a university professor I could not command that as local ministers could, and so I gradually decided that the best for me and my family was to save up and purchase a modest cottage or home in New England.

This became possible in a totally unexpected way. I had written a book, *Christian Deviations* (previously referred to), which first appeared in 1954 in London, but in its first ten years in England and the U.S.A. sold well over a hundred thousand copies, and by 1963 I was able to put down just over half the cost of a small, attractive cottage in Pittsfield, Vermont on Hawk Mountain. It now seems incredible that one could buy a new ski cottage for less than $17,000, but that only shows how inflation has increased. That solved the problem for summers, and, we could rent it to skiers and also visit it at Easter. It was the summer home of the family for twenty years, and from there the younger children went to earn their pocket-money as waiter and waitress in the hotels which surrounded the nearby major ski mountain in Vermont, namely Killington. For my purposes it had only one snag—apart from its inadequate weatherproofing—that was its distance of 45 miles to the nearest adequate College library, that of Dartmouth College in Hanover, New Hampshire.

My teaching at the university, as that of all the professors, united instruction of undergraduates in lectures and precepts, and the instruction of graduate students in seminars. The first undergraduate course that I gave paralleled the growth of English with North American Religious History from 1620 to the mid-twentieth century. It used to attract about 50 plus students regularly. I think that its attraction was due in part to the fact that several attending the course had fought in World War II or their parents had done so, hence there was a great interest in combining English with American History.

The syllabus will give the reader a clearer view of the development of the course. I began with the Anglican Middle Way between Roman Catholicism and Puritanism, then followed the Religious Settlements of the New World. Next came Civil War, Revolution, and the Restoration in England, followed by Progress and Problems in the American Colonies. The study of the Evangelical Revival in England led to naturally to The Great Awakenings in America.

Next we studied the Role of the Churches in an Independent America followed by Missions and Philanthropic Enterprises. The Expansion of Catholicism in England was matched by The Expanding Frontier, Immigration and Industrialization in North America. The Rise of Liberalism was looked at next, together with the Social and Racial Implications of the Christian Faith. The Proliferation of Sects was matched by the Growth of the Ecumenical Movement. The course ended with a consideration of The Present situation and of Prospects.

The second undergraduate course that I also taught in the early years was titled, "The Reformation and the Age of Reason." I inherited it from Paul Ramsey who rejoiced in being able, under the rubric of "the Age of Reason", to introduce the undergraduates to the subtleties of Immanuel Kant, and, as a Methodist, to the faith of the Wesley brothers. Before too long I changed the title and the development of the course to "The Protestant Reformation and the Catholic Counter-Reformation" thus providing an introduction to the living religion of the two major groups of Christians in the university. The change did not result in the attendance of fewer students and it enabled me to use my former studies of the Reformation together with a new emphasis on the vitality of the Catholic renewal.

Again I will supply a summary of a syllabus for greater clarification. I began with the actions and the theology of Luther which had precipitated the Reformation, the theology of Zwingli, and the exponents of the Radical Reformation, and dealt with Calvin as the systematic theologian of Protestantism, a controversial but magisterial figure, and with the Anglican Cranmer. Then I dealt with the Counter-Reformation as it proceeded in the Council of Trent, and in the creation of the Society of Jesus and Ignatius Loyola's vivid *Spiritual Exercises*, and the striking devotions of the Carmelite Order as developed by St. Teresa of Avila and St. John of the Cross.

My third undergraduate course was "Medieval Christian Thought" which, to my surprise, was highlighted in a "Special Course Evaluation Issue" of *The Daily Prince-*

tonian on April 22nd, 1959. This read: "Although the reading assignments are quite extensive and abstruse, Davies' lectures lend a strong guiding light to the understanding of life in the Christian Middle Ages." Then followed the kick: "Intensive treatment of Gothic cathedrals and neo-Thomist Jacques Maritain is considered unnecessary and redundant by many." My retort would have been that the cathedral is where religious life was celebrated and that Thomism was shown to be relevant by the most distinguished neo-Thomist philosopher who taught at Princeton, Jacques Maritain.

It may be of interest to describe this course. First I introduced the class to St. Augustine as an inquirer and as a finder of religious truth in his *Confessions*, continued with his magnificent interpretation of history while the Roman Empire was disintegrating in *The City of God,* and his understanding of Nature and Grace in a book of that title. Next we considered St. Anselm, the Archbishop of Canterbury, on Atonement in his *Cur Deus Homo* (Why God Became Man). Then followed St. Francis of Assisi, mystic and founder of the Friars Minor whose *The Little Flowers* and *The Mirror of Perfection* were read. We then devoted three weeks to St. Thomas Aquinas on the Attributes and the Grace of God and the Nature of Human Sin, followed by a study of his writing on Faith as well as on Hope and Charity. Here we had the advantage of using A. M. Fairweather's selection of Aquinas' *Summa Theologica* and for a lively biography, G. K. Chesterton's ironically titled book, *St. Thomas Aquinas, the Dumb Ox.* The final four weeks of the course reviewed the Medieval Synthesis as reflected in *Worship and Architecture*, while the class read Panofsky's *Gothic Architecture and Scholasticism.* (He was our neighbor at the Institute of Advanced Studies.) The Synthesis was also reflected in literature in the Christian Epic of Dante, and we read the *Inferno* and the *Paradiso.* Criticism of the synthesis was provided by reading William of Ockham. I ended by suggesting the relevance of medieval thought by requiring the students to read over fifty pages of *The Social and Political Philosophy* of Jacques Maritain edited by J. W. Evans and L. R. Ward. Instead of a mid-term test I required the undergraduates to prepare an essay on one aspect of the many-sided life of St. Bernard of Clairvaux, providing as examples of his preaching of the Crusade, as an ascetic, as confidant of rulers, and as a mystical writer. I proposed as a brief introduction to his life, Thomas Merton's, *The Last of the Fathers.*

Professors at Princeton were also expected to direct one Graduate Seminar each year. Until the arrival of a systematic theologian several years later when Arthur McGill came and after a few years left us for Harvard Divinity School, it seemed important to me to provide historical theology as the nearest substitute. For this reason I planned a seminar on "Major Modern Theologians" requiring the students to study Schleiermacher's *The Christian Faith*, Ritschl's *Justification and Reconciliation,* and Karl Barth's profound analysis in *Protestant Thought from Rousseau to Ritschl,* with appropriate selections from his monumental *Church Dogmatics.* In my attempt to be fair to each author if may be worth mentioning some of the questions I directed at the graduate students as they evaluated Barth. "Barth's theology has been described as (a) the theology of crisis, (b) dialectical theology, (c) the theology of paradox, and (d) the theology of the Word of God. Which is the most adequate description of the four?"

Other questions were: "Why did it take so long for his work to penetrate the Protestant world?" Who, among prior theologians have influenced him most: Kierkegaard, Calvin, Luther, Paul, Jeremiah?" What are Barth's theological pet aversions?" (The answer expected was process theology, and the failure to distinguish God from humanity in moralism, humanism, modernism, and fundamentalism.) Another seminal question was: "Where does Barth warrant criticism?" Finally I asked: "What are Barth's strengths?" These I felt were: The rigorous Biblical basis of theology, without fundamentalism; an unwillingness to dilute God's demands; a return to the Reformation concepts of justification by faith and reconciliation, and, finally, in an era of totalitarianism a claim that although theology is not humanis-

tic, yet it does defend humanitarianism as was manifested
in the historic Synod of Barmen.

Early on I led a graduate seminar on "Authority in
the Reformation" while studying Luther's three Treatises of
1520, Zwingli's the *Clarity and Certainty of the Word of
God* and *Of the Education of Youth,* Book IV of Calvin's
Institutes, and Hooker's *A Treatise on the Laws of Ecclesiastical Polity.* Once again the question was to raise the
importance of the Bible, the Church, Tradition and Experience as authorities, and to test the theologians for consistency, as well as for relevance in their day and ours.

The inevitable question arises: How did your
Princeton students compare with your Oxford students? At
the undergraduate level the Princeton students were not as
widely book-learned as their opposite numbers in Oxford,
but by their fourth year they had caught up to the third year
Oxonians, and were often more daring and less hesitant in
proposing new projects or new ways of assessing traditional viewpoints. The Oxford students seemed cautious, the
Princeton students more intellectuallly adventurous. But, of
course, this is a mere generalization, and there were brilliant and average students on both sides of the Atlantic.

It might be worth considering the fuller impressions
of the American people after we had lived a few years
amongst them in the elegant small city of Princeton, which
after all has had not seven centuries of history reflected in
its buildings as Oxford has. But Oxford also had what its
poet Gerald Manley Hopkins called "a base and brickish
skirt" which is baser because of the impact of Morris Mo-
tors, whereas all Princeton streets are lined with trees many
of them flowering in the Spring with cherry blossoms or
even what I had not seen since leaving South Africa, the
purple jacarandas.

For one thing the American way of eating was different from the English, and an American might well add,
"And a very good thing, too." There is a point in a joke Professor Ramsey told me, asserting that the difference between Heaven and Hell is not that of temperature but of the
tasks undertaken by members of different nationalities. In

Heaven the Italians are the lovers, but in Hell the Swiss. In Heaven the English are the police, but in Hell the Germans. In Heaven the Germans are the mechanics, but the French in Hell. In Heaven the Swiss are the organizers, but in Hell the Italians. Then came the punch line directed at me: in Heaven the French are the cooks, *and in Hell the English*! Thus, reader, you have been warned to challenge my generalizations.

The differences as I found them were as follows. The main meal of the day is taken in the evening, especially by commuters, while in England it was taken at noonday. American meals seemed to be much more piquantly flavored, although I was surprised by the near universality of tomato ketchup. Furthermore, salad was regarded as an absolute necessity whether as a side plate or as a garnishing, which was not the case in England. Coffee almost always supplants tea, even though the Elizabethan, Sir Walter Raleigh, discovered tea in North America. American tables are always illuminated by candles. But the United States is also very much the land of fast and often instant foods, rushed meals, hamburgers or hot dogs, and plentiful ice cream. What I found strange was that Europeans use the knife in the right hand and the fork in the left hand as pushers, while Americans cut with the knife in the right hand and then drop it, replacing it with the fork as a pusher to get the food into the mouth. It seemed unnecessarily awkward. Also, I found the quantities of food greater than I had been used to, and there seemed to be a mania for sandwiches as if life was a perpetual picnic.

Other differences included the great desire to make the stranger feel at home. Here was a welcome such as I would not have received in England. At first I was surprised by the immediacy of the use of the first names, whereas only relations and close friends did that in England. What was even more astonishing was the great kindness of Americans to neighbors in difficulty, as I was to experience it many years later when we had rented our house for the summer and I suddenly had to have a major operation. Immediately one faculty neighbor offered us a bedroom in their house, and a schoolteacher colleague of my wife began the family vacation earlier and left for their Vermont house to leave their Princeton home for our family to occupy. A smaller kindness was typical: when one of our children expressed a plebeian desire for fish and chips, the wife of a New Testament professor provided him instantly with crabmeat and crisps. Americans' great generosity can be seen in the vast number of charities they support worldwide.

The major criticism I would make of life in the U.S.A. is that the great majority of Americans even in prosperous times work far too hard, sometimes taking on two or three jobs, and find the benefits in richer houses, cars, clothing, and vacations irresistible in climbing the social ladder. My objection is not to them working hard, but to their dubiety about spending time off. They have an almost fanatical fear of leisure in which conversation and lengthy walks can flourish. How different is European love of peregrinations in the country, with walks in the parks here being briefer and only secondbest alternatives. Also, I miss the untimed postprandial conversations laced with wit and whimsy that delighted me in England. It seems never to have occurred to my fellow Americans that they can be far too serious! But this single defect, which foreigners attribute to the impact of Puritanism since secularized, is more than compensated for by their many qualities.

My work must have been fairly satisfactory because I received two distinctions in 1969. First, I was named Henry W. Putnam Professor of Religion with an increased salary. I was amused to hear from the new President of Princeton University, Dr. Robert Goheen, the story of how Princeton came to receive the Putnam munificence. The donor was not, apparently, a university man but admired the universities. He invited four golfing friends to tell him about their Colleges or Universities, and one failed to turn up. Luckily for myself the Princeton golfing partner arrived for the meeting, and the generosity was divided equally between the educational institutions of the three who were on the golf links.

The second form of recognition was the award of a prestigious J. S. Guggenheim Memorial Fund Fellowship for 1959-1960. In applying for this award I had proposed a research project which eventually would occupy me for fifteen years. When I had been writing *The Worship of the English Puritans* from the sixteenth to the eighteenth century it became clear to me that the development of worship in England was a dialogue—often carried on in the harshest tones—between Puritans and Anglicans, and that the best way to write liturgical history was to consider all the options. So I proposed writing what became eventually Volume III of a five-volume series, *Worship and Theology in England*, which Princeton and Oxford University Presses would publish with biographical and architectural illustrations. I was thus carrying on the research I had begun at Oxford but with wider ramifications and an ecumenical approach. I included consideration of hymnology and music and architecture, and delved wherever possible into primary sources, which is why I had to go to England for my research. This was carried on in 1960 in Cambridge University Library with occasional visits to the British Museum (now Library) in London. I chose Cambridge because my doctoral dissertation supervisor, Edward Ratcliff, was now a University Professor at Cambridge University, and it seemed narrowing to act as if Oxford was the only major university in Great Britain. I should also point out here that Princeton University for many years supported this research, not only by granting me sabbatical semesters every four years at full pay, but also providing continuing summer grants for travel to and from England and a subsidy for the charges for board and lodging. In this way I was able to write five comprehensive volumes in this series, with access to sources, and had the opportunity to consult with leading liturgiologists when necessary, and especially for the development of theology and worship in the present century. Such generosity I had not met with academically in South Africa or in England.

8

RESEARCH AND ITS RESULTS:
1960 - 1984

The American slogan "Publish or Perish" is a powerful incentive to research especially to those in the lower echelons of the scholastic hierarchy, and who need to publish books to advance from being Assistant Professors to Associate Professors with the probability of tenure. I had found it difficult to make time for research at Oxford, except during the summer, because I had tutorials that used up in both Mansfield and Regent's Park Colleges the best part of fifteen to twenty hours a week, with Sunday services extra and this did not include lectures or the preparation of them. The lighter Princeton lecturing load, combined with preceptorials, accounted for about ten hours per week, to which could be added two hours for advising, adding up to a dozen hours per week in all. This left ample time for thorough research. It might seem odd, however, that my main research work was in the area of liturgics, which would seem more appropriate in a theological seminary than in a university Department of Religion. I doubt if I should have devoted as much time as I did to the study of worship, but for two considerations.

The first was that although Protestantism thought homiletics, the study of preaching, was far more important than worship, yet a sermon only used one third of the time spent during an hour of worship each Sunday, and I felt it was important to study the significant context of worship, with the varied types of prayers, the hymnody, and the increasingly important celebration of the sacraments of Baptism and the Eucharist or Lord's Supper. Furthermore, by the courtesy of the President of Princeton Theological Seminary, Dr. James I. McCord, and the Professor of Homiletics, Dr. Donald Macleod, I was invited every alternate year to give a series of lectures there on the history of Christian worship, Roman Catholic, Orthodox, and Protestant.The arrangement was that I would have two teaching hours per week reduced from my university load for which the Seminary would pay the University. In return, the Seminary would invite me to teach for the first three weeks of their Summer Institute with remuneration. Thus I had every inducement to go on researching ecumenically while teaching students from many different denominations at the seminary, and ministers of many denominations in the summer. Furthermore, while it was usual for liturgiologists to downgrade preaching, I always considered the proclamation of the Gospel as an essential part of every worship service, and my research always included analyses of the theology of worship and the characteristics of preaching and the nature of sacred rhetoric in every century I studied. It was with a determination to write the history of worship in every major Christian denomination in England through the five centuries from the Reformation to the present that I came to Cambridge to begin the task. My historical series was titled, *Worship and Theology in England.*

It was during the seven months in Cambridge that I was able to revise the manuscript of Volume III of my series, sub-titled *From Watts and Wesley to Maurice,* and undertake a more thorough comparison of the two great English evangelists of the eighteenth century, George Whitefield the original field-preacher whose sonorous voice (as computed by Benjamin Franklin) could be heard by 30,000 people in Philadelphia was remarkably persuasive, and John Wesley whose preaching was simple, logical, lucid, and practical. I was able to compare the remarkable hymns composed by Issac Watts and Charles Wesley. I was also glad to have the time to study the Christian Socialists of the mid-nineteenth century of whom the most notable theological exponent was F. D. Maurice and their best novelist, Charles Kingsley. On my return this manuscript was accepted by Princeton University Press and published in 1961.

The making of the successor volume, sub-titled, *From Newman to Martineau 1850-1900* was undertaken while at Cambridge. In the course of that year I was able to interview the Regius Professor Divinity in Cambridge University (Dr. E. C. Ratcliff), the Revd. Cyril Bowles (the Principal of Ridley Hall, an evangelical Anglican College), the Very Revd. F. W. Dillistone, the Dean of Liverpool Cathedral who kindly invited me to preach there, the Revd. Dr. Gilbert Cope, a keen liturgiologist at the University of Birmingham, and Principal John Marsh of Mansfield College, Oxford. I also wanted to be sure that I was interpreting the art and architecture of the eighteenth and nineteenth centuries accurately. My advisors were Dr. Peter Murray of the Courtauld Institute of Art in London University,- and an old friend, Mr. H. V. Molesworth Roberts of the Library of the Royal Institute of British Architects.

As a spur to my research in Cambridge I was invited by the Faculty of Divinity there to give a series of lectures on a theme of my own choice. So in the Spring of 1960 I spoke on the lives and the sermons of John Henry Newman, F. W. Robertson of Brighton, R. W. Dale of Birmingham, and C. H. Spurgeon of London, respectively, Anglican becoming Roman Catholic, Anglican, Congregationalist, and Baptist. These lectures were the first draft of what became the final chapter of the book, "The Power of the Victorian Pulpit", 66 pages in length. There were also chapters on Presbyterian Worship, Scottish and English, the Catholic Trend in Anglican Worship, the Renascence of Roman Catholic Worship, the Liturgical Pioneers among the Baptists and the Congregationalists, and the Worship of the New Dissenters, Methodists and Unitarians. I also included an account of Ecclesial Architecture: From Neo-Grecian to Neo-Gothic. Volume IV appeared in 1962, when I had time to revise the first draft almost completed in

1961, because by being made a Senior Fellow of the Council of Humanities my teaching load was reduced and my research time increased.

The seven months in Cambridge offered many delights: walking past the Colleges, especially the trio of King's (with its superb Gothic Chapel in which a magnificent Rubens Nativity scene had recently been placed), Trinity, and St. John's, and boating on the Backs. At the end of March I entrained to Coventry partly to see the new Cathedral there, but also to take delivery of a new Jaguar saloon. I was a little apprehensive since my only previous Jaguar car (a second-hand one) had broken down in the main street of Princeton and stopped traffic at a popular corner, but the new automobile behaved as it should for the rest of our stay. On Sunday May 8th, I preached at Liverpool's modern neo-Gothic Anglican Cathedral and was taken by Dean Dillistone up into the tower, quaking, because I have a fear of heights which I did not wholly succeed in hiding.

Another interesting preaching invitation came my way. That was to preach the University Sermon on Ascension Day in Great Saint Mary's Church, Cambridge. It was preceded by an invitation to lunch by the eminent historian, Professor Herbert Butterfield, Master of Peterhouse, and Vice-Chancellor of the University. The topic was one that I had not pondered on deeply and it presented difficulties which I acknowledged in the pulpit. I observed that one poet had lamented the disappearance of the three-storied medieval world affirming that "the heavens have grown afar off and become astronomical" and that Pascal, with characteristic honesty declared, "The silence of these infinite spaces frightens me." Despite these difficulties I argued that the evolutionary view of creation can provide a greater sense of the infinite patience of God, as well as of God's mystery. Sir James Jeans, the Cambridge scientist in his book *The Mysterious Universe* provided an admirable analogy of the time-scale on which God works. If we think of the tower, Cleopatra's needle, a penny and a postage stamp, then from Cleopatra's needle God was creating the world, the penny's thickness represented the time of prehistoric animals, and the thinness of a postage stamp the time since humans appeared on the scene. Astronomically and technologically this is a new world. One Marxist poet, thinking of much valetudinarian and conservative piety on the part of Christians wrote: "There stands the Church blocking out the Sun." It could well be true, I added, that this obscures the Son of Righteousness, the eternal Son of God who was a carpenter.

I also pointed out that the Ascension is omitted from Matthew and is peripheral in Mark, because the great new facts of the Gospel were the Resurrection of the crucified Messiah and the Universal presence of the Holy Spirit with the people of God at and after Pentecost. Yet there are two lessons for Ascension Day. There is the *Sursum corda*—we should lift up our hearts by the gift of faith. There is also a rebuke: "Men of Galilee, why do you stand looking into heaven? This Jesus who was taken up from you into heaven will come in the same way as you saw him go into heaven." God's rebukes and judgments are the chastisements of His holy love; so let the judgments have their effect before God's Final Judgment at the end of history, and rejoice that His promises cannot fail.

We went down at Easter to my parents in the Isle of Jersey off the French coast, continued for a few days in Paris, and after the briefest stay in Basle, joined an English touring group at Genoa, and thence went to Pisa, Florence, Siena, Rome, Rimini, Ravenna, Padua, and Venice, returning via Verona and Milan, then through France. Of that month's holiday my memories are of the high and dangerous mountain roads on which our driver took our bus, the superb paintings of Botticelli and Michelangelo in the Uffizi Gallery in Florence, the pageantry of the Papal procession at St. Peter's, Rome, and the ceiling that Michelangelo painted in extreme discomfort upside down, and the wonderful waterscape of Venice and its grand cathedral of St. Mark's approached by a huge square on which there were more pigeons than I had ever seen together.

In France, the most moving sight for me, apart from
the rose-windows of Notre Dame, was the Sainte Chapelle,
with its lovely stained-glass lancet windows, built by King
Louis IX (Saint Louis) to house the relics of the crown of
thorns, parts of the true cross, and the holy lance, all obtained during a crusade. It is hard to imagine a lovelier setting for ancient buildings than the Ile de la Cité, as holy island, surrounded by the waters of the Seine, where so many
attractive walks can be taken. We were glad to take advantage of the historic beauty and culture of Europe, which we
had missed in North America, and to visit our relatives
again.

The third book which was Vol. V. of my series,
Worship and Theology in England, appeared in 1965, because I received a rarely awarded second Guggenheim Memorial Fund Fellowship in 1964-65 which made possible
an extensive study of the twentieth century varieties of
English Worship. The book itself, with the sub-title, *The
Ecumenical Century 1900-1965*, by dint of summer researches in England and the first half of 1965 at Oxford,
could not possibly have been produced without the benefit
of many experts whom I was privileged to interview in
England. Since the Second Vatican Council had made such
prodigious changes in worship as codified in "The Constitution of the Sacred Liturgy" in order to guarantee the maximum participation of the people in worship, there was a
simplification, clarification, and purification of the rites of
the liturgy it seemed right to the end the book in 1965.
Three changes in particular show how important the revi-
sion of the Roman Rite was: the insistence upon translation
from Latin into the vernacular language, the provision of
four alternate forms of celebration of the Liturgy instead of
the previous single formulary, with one form clearly mod-
eled on that of the Eastern Orthodox Churches. Furthermore, if imitation is the sincerest form of flattery, the other
churches were happy to take leaves out of the book of the
new Roman liturgical practice.

In dealing with three handmaids of worship, religious art, music and architecture, I was happy to be able to call upon the advice of experts and enjoyed three interviews with Lady Kathleen Epstein on the work of the late Sir Jacob Epstein, and also the immense learning of the Revd. Erik R. Routley who had made the wide field of Sacred Music his own, especially in the area of hymnology. It was also a great pleasure to be invited to stay as the guest of the famous Benedictine Community of Downside, where the Abbot, the Right Reverend B. Christopher Butler, gave me the benefit of his inside knowledge of Vatican II. Others who helped to guide me were the Revd. Principal John Marsh whose Oxford home was mine for Michaelmas term, and I shared it with an old friend, the Revd. Dr. Robert S. Paul, who had been Associate Director of the Ecumenical Institute of the World Council of Churches in Switzerland, with whom I was able to discuss some of the more controversial questions. Principal Marsh also had the inside track on recent developments in Worship in the Congregational Churches. A similar service was performed by the Revd. R. Aled Davies, Convener of the Presbyterian Church of England's Assembly Committee on Public Worship. The Revd. Dr. Ernest A. Payne, a good Free Church historian, gave me similar assistance about Baptist worship, as the Secretary of the Baptist Union of Churches. Dr. Mortimer Rowe, the former General Secretary of the Unitarian and Free Christian Churches of Great Britain, gave much help by his lengthy letters and his loan of rare books. Professor Ratcliff also advised me. With all this advice it became easier to avoid the great pitfalls of writing almost contemporary where disagreements seem to cover quiet congruence with thick black clouds of smoke.

I tried to clarify the situation by dividing the research into two very different but complementary sections. The first was termed "The Wide Angle View" and the second was "The Narrow Focus." In the first part I had chapters on The Continental Liturgical Movement and its influence, on The Rebirth of Religious Architecture and Art (which included a study of five new cathedrals, and of the three painters: Spencer, Sutherland, and Piper, as well as of three sculptors: Gill, Epstein, and Henry Moore). The third chapter dealt with the development of Church Music, whether experimental, or light church music, and the importance of the newer hymnody and psalmody. The fourth chapter expounded the early development of theology until 1933, describing the fundamental points of Bishop Gore and Archbishop Temple, and the Free Churchmen Forsyth and Oman. The fifth chapter explored the return to orthodoxy (without Biblical inerrancy), the rediscovery of the Church, the concern for a Christian Sociology, and the Cambridge Christian Radicals. The sixth chapter, and the last of part I analyzed Trends and Types of Preaching. It included Apologetical preaching illustrated by Bishop Hensley Henson, the Psychological type expressed by Leslie D. Weatherhead, the philosophical theologian as preacher exemplified by Professor H. H. Farmer, the evangelical "Great-heart" Dr. W. E. Sangster, the Charismatic type of preaching in "Woodbine Willie and Dick Sheppard; and the notable liturgical preacher who combined wit and wisdom, Fr. Ronald Knox.

Part II chronicled the progress of the liturgical Movement amongst Catholics, Anglican Worship before and after the crisis of 1928, the Worship of the Free Churches, that of the Society of Friends, and of the Unitarian Churches. The final chapter XIII, was a Concluding Critique which noted and evaluated area of agreement and of disagreement. Up to this point the longest book in the series, almost five hundred pages, it was by far the most difficult to write.

Shortly after the publication of the third volume in the series two honors came my way which testified to the general ecumenical appreciation of these works, and made the effort seem very worthwhile. The first was the gracious award in 1966 made by a Catholic College in Philadelphia, now La Salle University, of the honorary degree of Doctor of Letters. Church history had changed! The address explaining why the degree was awarded was written by and read aloud by a Dominican Father, who centuries before would have traduced me before the Inquisition! And in

1970 I was granted the earned Doctorate of Letters (D.Litt.) of Oxford University for the same three volumes that had appeared.

There were however two further volumes to appear, numbers I and II. Part of this work had been done for the Free Churches in my original Oxford doctoral dissertation *The Worship of the English Puritans* (1948) which, as I indicated in the Preface, might equally well have been named "The Free Church Tradition of Christian Worship in England. . ." I still had to trace the worship of the Roman Catholic and Anglican Churches in England from 1534 to 1603, which I did in Volume I subtitled, *From Cranmer to Hooker* and in the Volume II, *From Andrewes to Baxter and Fox. 1603-1690.*

In 1534 the English Church had broken away from the international Catholic Church, forming an autonomous national community, the Church of England. Hence Volume I was devoted to its origin and early development, its theological debates with Catholics and Puritans, and its early expressions of worship in two important editions of the Book of Common Prayer; which have become the chief channels of the doctrine and devotion of the Anglican communion worldwide for four centuries. The first chapter dealt with the controversy between Catholics and Anglicans, the second between Puritans and Anglicans, the third concentrated on the important Eucharistic Controversy and the four theories fighting for recognition. This concluded the historical and theological first part of the book.

The second part dealt exclusively with the Liturgical Alternatives. Catholic worship was analyzed in the light of the reforms of the Council of Trent in one chapter. A second dealt with the Anglican Prayer Books of 1549 and 1552. The third considered Anglican preaching. Two chapters were devoted to Puritan Worship and Puritan Preaching. The Worship of the Separatists was also considered. The third part of the book dealt with Liturgical Arts and Aids. One chapter dealt with Religious Architecture and Art, a second with Church Music, and a final chapter with

Spirituality.

The divines whom I had sketched, in this book were Archbishop Cranmer, John Jewel, and Richard Hooker, all Anglicans, Sir and Saint Thomas More and Edmund Campion, both English Catholics, and William Perkins, the leading Puritan theologian, together with cameos of several others of slightly less importance. I counted on the help of most of those scholars who had assisted me before, with the addition of the expertise in Art and Architecture of my son Hugh. This book appeared in 1970 and the research was done during summers in Oxford and the larger part of a year spent at the congenial Henry Huntington Library, in San Marino, California. I have never researched in a more attractive setting. The magnificent gardens in which the Research Fellows are free to roam (for short periods, of course) in the sunshine amid the roses, flowering trees, cacti, and other forms of vegetation, the attractive dining room in which the scholars meet for repasts and conversations, as well as the two excellent museums, one specializing in English art and the other in American art, are unimaginably delightful. Our residence during these months was not San Marino, for only the ultra-wealthy live there for the most part, but in neighboring Pasadena in a modern apartment. My single surprise at the Huntington was at the relative paucity of scholars considering the vastness of its literary and aesthetic resources. But in the afternoons, both Museums and Gardens were filled with delighted tourists.

My last volume, Volume II in the series, was subtitled, *From Andrewes to Baxter and Fox*, since I intended to emphasize the contributions to worship made by the High Anglican, Bishop Lancelot Andrewes, as by the learned Puritan divine, Richard Baxter, and the founder of the Society of Friends, the Quaker John Fox. This volume appeared in 1975 and was the longest of all extending to 592 pages. When this was completed my good-natured colleagues in the Department of Religion made ironical reference to my "pentateuch." It was a relief to have completed so long a project, that had taken fifteen years of my life.

The analysis was an investigation of the theological and liturgical traditions of Anglicanism, Puritanism, and Sectarianism, as well as of Roman Catholicism. Part I discussed ecclesiologies, church architecture, spirituality as a preparation for public worship, and the role of preaching. Part II examined cultic controversies over prayer, vestments, ceremonies, music, holy days, and the sacramental presence of Christ. Part III described the formal aspect of worship, analyzing the Service Books of the major denominations. A concluding survey and critique evaluated the strengths and weaknesses of Liturgical Worship and of Free Church Worship, and their ultimate complementarity.

I had been researching in the summers at Oxford and had met a new companion and helper, Marie-Hélène, then professor of English at the University of Paris-X, who was also researching in the Renaissance and whom I was eventually to marry. In 1972 my former wife and I went through a traumatic divorce for which I was mainly responsible. It was also the recognition of a failure in human relations in which we both shared. Brenda loved music, whereas I sacrificed my ears to my eyes and visual art. Brenda's training was in the rearing and educating of small children at which she was expert. My professional interests were almost exclusively concerned with students from the ages of eighteen to thirty. To me the saddest feature is that I had found a splendid new friend who shared my literary and historical enthusiasms to the full, but Brenda did not. To say more on this topic might be hurtful to my former wife and our children, so I will desist.

The ultimate recognition for these five volumes came in the Berakah Award of the North American Academy of Liturgy in 1979. This major award was presented by Professor James F. White, with the inscription: "As a historian of worship and theology in England, he has written a chronicle unequaled in scope and insight of the liturgical life and thought of a whole people over the course of five hundred years." The most thorough analyses of the five volumes were written by two of the most eminent liturgiologists in the United States, the first an Episcopalian, Professor Massey Shepherd, Jr., and the second by Professor James F. White, a Methodist. Shepherd's article, "Horton Davies' *Worship and Theology in England*." appeared in *The Journal of Religion*, vol. 58, No. 2: pp. 182-193, April 1978. White's article, entitled, "Writing the History of English Worship. The achievement of Horton Davies." came out in *Church History*, vol. 47, pp. 434-40, December 1978.

Later research was single-minded, not multiple-volume minded! In two cases they were the works of collaboration. In 1978 there appeared *Sacred Art in a Secular Century*. which my son Hugh and I prepared together. He handled the technique of art and I its theological character. This was published by my Benedictine friends of The Liturgical Press, Collegeville, Minnesota. The work was a study of religious art in the twentieth century. The Introduction dealt with the life, death, and rebirth of religious symbols. It was limited to art in the western hemisphere and it attempted to evaluate 74 different paintings, etchings, or sculptures done by 24 different artists from 8 different countries. It included the greatest religious artists of our times, notably the Jewish master, Marc Chagall, and the Catholic Master, Georges Rouault, as well as Emil Nolde and Sir Jacob Epstein It also studied the occasional religious work of such brilliant innovators as Picasso and Dali, Moore and Bacon, Derain, Lipchitz, Rothko and Newman. Impressive religious artists who deserved to be better known were also introduced, among them the painter, Sir Stanley Spencer, and the sculptor, Ernst Barlach, along with two notable women sculptors, Germaine Richier and Kaethe Kollwitz.

Chapter 1 dealt with Old Symbols Renewed and Revised. Here we considered traditional Jewish and Christian themes, such as Jacob wrestling with the Angel, the Madonna, the Crucifixion, and the Last Supper, seeing that some found new meanings in them. Chapter 2 was titled "Old Symbols syncretized or Secularized." Marc Chagall is an interesting example of syncretism, combining Jewish

and Christian apprehensions of the same symbol in a remarkable painting in which the Crucified Christ is central,
but He is surrounded by the symbols of the Holocaust in
both Germany and Russia. This, Chagall's "The White Crucifixion"' appeared in vivid color as our dustjacket. Chapter
3 introduced new symbols and emphases. Ernst Nolde has
depicted in a vivid way the children hugging Jesus, while
the displeased disciples are annoyed at this disturbance.
Max Beckmann's "Christ and the Woman taken in Adul-
tery" depicts a balding Christ with one arm directed towards the woman who kneels before him in supplication,
while the other arm fends off a rustic who is about to throw
a stone at her. Above is a supercilious Pharisee. Sir Stanley
Spencer locates Christ in his own village of Cookham-on-
Thames in several paintings, notably in a depiction of the
Last Supper, where Jesus breaks the bread in the form of
his own broken heart, anticipating the Crucifixion. One is
reminded of the relevance of Paul Tillich's apothegm: "A
Christ who is not contemporary is not the Christ."

The last chapter details evidence for a new religious
spirit and its signs. In this case the ethical evidence of the
impact of Religion is in the forefront, rather than the symbolism of Jewish or Christian events or their doctrinal
meaning. Picasso's *Guernica* is a prophetic denunciation of
the exploitation of humanity, of animals, and of nature with
its horrifying fragmentation of women, men, children, and
beasts. Rouault's unlovely prostitutes exhibit the ravages of
male lust, his pathetic poor the inhumanity of the grasping
and heedless rich, and his dejected prisoners, including
Christ, and his porcine judges, all document the perversion
of justice. A second characteristic is shown in a profound
sense of compassion, as in the tender picture of Picasso,
"Child with a Dove" or, more profoundly, in Rouault's famous "Sacred Face" with Christ's pinched cheeks and
hauntingly sad eyes which have plumbed the depths of mis-
ery for the love of humankind. The third characteristic of
recent painting appeared to be a correction of the first. It
was the rediscovery of joy in a century that desperately

needed it. It was notably expressed in the paintings of Chagall in his levitations of lovers, in Nolde's paintings of children dancing. and of the holy hilarity of Christ in "The Entry into Jerusalem", and in Matisse's Chapel of the Rosary
at Vence which caused a young Dominican sister to affirm
that it was the most joyful chapel in which she had ever
worshipped, and in which the aging artist returned to the
Faith.

The second collaborative book was the most joyful
to prepare because, it was the fruit of two traveling holidays in France. My second wife, Marie-Hélène, and I decided that it would be fun to write a book on the famous
medieval pilgrimage to Santiago of Compostela in Northwestern Spain, for which there were four routes through
France. It required two summers of traveling and several
summers of writing. To have walked as most of the medieval pilgrims did would have taken too long, and, so would
riding on horseback. So, through the kindness of Annick
L'Hoste, a colleague of my wife, we borrowed a four horse-
power Renault painted in a plaid of blue and green which
was economical on gas, and occasionally it had to be
pushed and pulled in thoroughly medieval fashion by huff-
ing and puffing villagers to the nearest car doctor.

We were fascinated by the mixture of motives that
determined pilgrims to make the long and hazardous journey. The highest motive was sanctity and the chance of a
fresh start in the religious life visiting the places associated
with the saints en route which kept their relics. It was a
temporary novitiate with its own dress and insignia. The-
chances of being buried in holy ground were greater, and
thus of reaching heaven if one died on pilgrimage. Some
pilgrims went to fulfill vows of family and friends, as it
could be undertaken by proxy. Indulgences were also a
magnetic attraction. Other boons sought were the restoration of physical health, exorcism from demon possession
and the gift of children for the infertile, all to be obtained
from the saints, the friends of God. There were also purely
secular motives: curiosity, new scenes, new faces, the desire for community, escape from the monotonous drudgery

of daily life, or running away from responsibilities. This consideration of motives gave us deeper appreciation of the Roman Catholic Church's genius in inspiring the saint as well as encouraging the man or woman in the street. It has provided the austere diet of the anchorite and the monk and the ampler fare needed by Chaucer's Wife of Bath.

Other parts of the book emphasized the strange allure of remote Compostela, Preparations for the Pilgrimage, and the attractions of the resplendent shrines and their relics. The Middle Ages had a lust for relics because the saints were the powerful friends and associates of Christ in heaven. When St. Hugh of Lincoln was a guest of the Abbey of Fécamp in France, he was allowed to see the arm of Saint Mary Magdalene, which was tightly wrapped in cloth and silk bandages which the monks had not dared to unwrap. Despite their furious objections, Saint Hugh cut off the wrappings with a knife and tried to break off a piece of the arm. Finding this too hard, he then tried to bite off a finger "first with his incisors, and finally with his molars" and thus he succeeded in breaking off two fragments which he handed for safe keeping to his biographer. His defense to the abbot was that if he handled the body of Christ in the Eucharist why shouldn't he treat the bones of the saints in the same way? Relics attracted pilgrims and brought great wealth to medieval monasteries.

We visited the great pilgrimage churches at Tours, Limoges, Conques, and Toulouse and the many sanctoral centers in Provence at Arles, formerly the primatial see of Gaul, where the Church of St. Trophime can be seen. Near Arles is Alyscamps where there are over a thousand marble tombs amid cypresses, where the holy dead repose. We also made a deviation to the south to Saint Guilhelm-du-Désert, a church commemorating one of the generals of Charlemagne, who took monastic vows at fifty, established the monastery and gave it a relic of the true Cross which had been given to him by Charlemagne. This we saw placed in the center of a reliquary cross. The only reliquary which could compare with this for importance would be the crown of thorns for which Saint Louis created the Sainte Chapelle of Paris. Pilgrims not going to the Holy Land could hardly come physically closer to the Savior.

A second route to Compostela began at Le Puy and was chiefly frequented by Burgundians and Germans. This would lead to St. Foy at Conques. At both churches there were famous relics. Le Puy had one thorn from the crown of thorns, but Conques in its abbey church dedicated to St. Faith retains the most significant survival of the great medieval treasures of France. The eyes of pilgrims must have been dazzled by these marvels of the jeweller's and goldsmith's arts. The so-called "majesty" of St. Foy is carved of wood and covered with gold and begemmed with pearls, intaglios and rock crystal. This crowned image, with jeweled ear-rings, sits on a throne surmounted by rock, crystal balls, and her enamel eyeballs present a penetrating gaze, and were probably intended to recall a famous act of healing in which she restored the sight of a blind suppliant whose eyes had been torn out by the roots. Certainly her church was thronged with those who had maladies of the eyes and other sicknesses. We were also delighted to visit the Abbey church of St. Peter of Moissac. It had a glorious tympanum on the southern porch revealing the twenty-four elders of the apocalypse worshipping Jesus Christ in glory, playing their lutes and viols in melodious adoration.

The third route for pilgrims began at Vezelay with stations at Saint Martial of Limoges, Saint Leonard of Noblat, and Saint Front of Périgueux. Vézelay Church, from which Saint Bernard preached the second Crusade is a magnificent Romanesque church with a superb curved inner arch over two doors which depicts a regal Christ blessing the apostles beneath, while sending them on their missionary tasks, all carved in golden stone. Practically nothing remained of the great church of Saint Martial of Limoges apart from some illuminated manuscripts, and Saint Front of Perigueux has been so renovated that it is more modern than medieval.

The fourth route for Compostela pilgrims began at Orléans, although it must have been joined by pilgrims from the coastal Mont-Saint-Michel and from England, and from Saint-Denis and Chartres. Chartres boasted the tunic worn by the Virgin at the Annunciation and still displays it. Orléans claimed a part of the True Cross. The next stations were Poitiers, where Charles Martel finally overthrew the Invading Saracens, and Saintes. Several shrines in France are associated with the *Chanson de Roland* where the great Paladin fought bravely but vainly against the Saracens (but actually against the Basques). His body was supposed to rest at Saint Romain of Blaye and his famous horn was kept at Saint Seurin of Bordeaux. These heroes were treated as saints because they were fighting for the Christian faith. The two most important names and influences on the Compostela Pilgrimage are Charlemagne and Cluny. The first generously donated the most precious relics he had purchased from the Christian Emperor of Byzantium, and under the inspiration of the second many daughter abbeys were built to house these relics.

I have already mentioned some of the sculptures we witnessed on our journey, but the most memorable were at Moissac and Souillac, and also at Autun near to Vézelay. A capital at the latter reveals the Virgin Mary in her frail and enchanting beauty, while at Moissac we saw a huge Jeremiah with dominating eyes and a strong curved hand staring at us from the side of the doorway, and Souillac has the equally dramatic prophet Isaiah.

The goal of medieval pilgrims was the cathedral church of Compostela. It has three remarkable sculptured façades. The northern face displayed the Creation and the Incarnation, the southern the manifestation of Christ to the world, and the western His glorious triumph. The western front was the work of Master Matthew, a genius, which radiates elation, manifesting Christ's triumph and the joy of the elect in heaven. A huge Christ is preparing to show His wounds. To his right, supported by two angels, is a vast Cross—the instrument of His glory and of the redemption of His mystical Body, the Church, which surrounds Him. The almost forty companions of Christ are on their knees with hands joined in the attitude of prayer as they enjoy the vision of God in ecstasy. The archivolt is occupied by the twenty-four elders of the Book of Revelation seated about the throne, with their heads crowned and each holding a bowl in one hand and a harp in the other. Appropriately, Saint James of Compostela appears on the central trumeau supporting the tympanum. His face bears a striking resemblance to that of Christ, and in his hand is the staff of pilgrimage. Eventually the pilgrims reached home to receive new honors from their kith and kin and friends. And we ended our book with these lines: "They were better prepared for the last pilgrimage of all through the dark doors of death to where Christ and his friends (and theirs), the saints, held unending festival in everlasting light, not in the field of one star (*Campus stellae*) but beyond the Milky Way with all the stars ablaze."

The book was published in 1982 by the Associated University Presses, and it was dedicated to our oldest friend in Princeton, Mrs. Dorothy Thomas, as delightful as she is devout and hospitable.

In this long record of researches I would like to finish with reference to another project which gave me great delight and which I produced on a National Endowment of the Humanities Fellowship at the Huntington Library in Southern California. My wife, Marie-Hélène, was at the same time writing a biography of an imaginative novelist, also a Presbyterian minister, Frederick Buechner. It was a joy for me to renew the friendships made on the previous visit, and these included Leland Carlson, one of the very few American historians of English Dissenting religion. We were introduced to the zestful Mexican drink, Margarita, by John and Hannah Demaray, both professors of English literature. Other friends were Dr. James Thorp and his wife, Betty, whom we had known when he was one of the Deans of the Graduate School at Princeton University, Dr. Hallet Smith and his wife were particularly kind to us as were Dr. and Mrs. Hardacre, whose daughter Helen was a colleague of mine at Princeton and an expert in Japanese Religious Studies.

Another contact gave us great delight, meeting the Revd. Dr. Howard Happ, whose doctoral dissertation at Princeton was done partly under my direction, a very amusing man, whimsical and witty, and who eventually became President of the Northridge College of the State University in California.

While at the Huntington Library from October 1981 to June 1982 I researched on the English Metaphysical Preachers of the period from 1588 to 1645. The most famous of whom was the witty John Donne, ultimately Dean of St. Paul's Cathedral, London, and a brilliant poet as well as preacher. When I was awarded the Fellowship for this research I had proposed to undertake a comparative study of three Metaphysical Preachers, John Donne the Roman Catholic who converted to Anglicanism, George Herbert who was always an Anglican, and Richard Crashaw, an Anglican who converted to Roman Catholicism, all of whom were distinguished English poets. It was a great surprise to find on reaching the Huntington Library that there were no surviving sermons of either Herbert or Crashaw, least of all collected editions of them as in the case of Donne. So I had to bestir myself to find other Metaphysical Preachers with whom to compare Donne.

Again to my surprise I found about forty in all, whose sermons had survived in print. It was interesting to discover that a few were more renowned than Donne as preachers in his time. It had been assumed that all metaphysical preachers were Arminians, but four of the most famous were consistent Calvinists. They were Henry Smith (known as the "silver-tongued" for his oratory), Thomas Adams who was styled "the prose Shakespeare of Puritan theologians", as well as Bishops John Hackett and Ralph Brownrig. Up to then Puritan preachers had been thought to avoid shows of learning and wit and to cultivate the plain style.

It soon became my task to particularize the distinctive characteristics of the metaphysical style. I finally concluded that there were eleven in all. They were: wit, patristic learning, classical lore, citations from Greek and Latin, and occasionally Hebrew originals; illustrations from "unnatural" natural history; allegorical exegesis; sermon plans with complex divisions and sub-divisions; a Senecan and staccato style; the use of paradoxes, riddles, and emblems; a fondness for speculation; and the relation of doctrinal and devotional preaching to the Christian calendar. It was also my conclusion that it was the classical education in the leading English schools, requiring pupils to translate Latin and Greek verse into English verse that was the single major factor accounting for the metaphysical style in poetry and preaching. It became clear also that James I and Charles I were great admirers of wit and learning and that they chose royal chaplains for these qualities; learning made them good defenders of the Christian faith, and wit kept the captive congregations at court intrigued. I gave equal attention to the biographies of the preachers, the themes of their sermons, and the techniques of sermon construction and preaching, with separate, chapters on learning and eloquence, wit and imagery, and the uses to which they were put. The title of the book recalled in part Donne's admiring friend who wrote in his epitaph for Donne that he preached like an angel from a cloud, but with his feet in none: *Like Angels from a Cloud: The English Metaphysical Preachers 1588-1645*. It was, published by the Huntington Library, San Marino in 1986, an honor since they only select four books to publish each year. It was beautifully printed and bound, and Dr. Guilland Sutherland of the Library staff, its editor, had provided an attractive seventeenth century ideogram cover showing an angel with two trumpets blowing from a cloud.

Since the book appeared two years after my retirement from Princeton University I thankfully dedicated it:

> For my congenial colleagues,
> past and present
> in the pioneering Department
> of Religion in Princeton
> University.

I had two further advantages before it was published. One was the invitation to direct a seminar at the Folger Shakespeare Library in Washington, D. C. on the theme of the Metaphysical Preachers in the Fall of 1982. Its dozen members, comprised professors of English literature in universities or colleges and doctoral candidates in the same field. It was a most stimulating experience to try out my various chapters on them for their reactions and this led, undoubtedly to greater clarity in my presentation in the book. I also gave a lecture at the Folger Library entitled, "At Their Wits' End: The English Metaphysical Preachers." The wit, at least, was greatly appreciated, if not the theology!

9

TEACHING AND ADMINISTRATION:
1965-1984

Chapter 7 described three courses I taught undergraduates for several years, but I now want to describe two
later courses which correlated my three major interests:
Christianity, Literature and Visual Art.

The course on fiction was entitled "Religious Ideas
in Literature." Since it included writers from other than
Christian perspectives in Religion it involved collaboration
with my colleagues who were experts in Asian Religions as
well as in Judaism. It varied considerably from year to year
in the choice of books to be analyzed and in the expertise of
my different colleagues. In 1973, for example, William La-
Fleur, an expert in Japanese religion, and Karen Lindsley, a
specialist on Christian religious poetry assisted me. Bill La-
Fleur lectured on Wu Ch'eng-en's, *The Monkey*, Han-Shan's
Cold Mountain, Yuasa's *The Year or My Life,* Kawabata's
Snow Country, Hesse's *Siddhartha*, and Saigyo's *Poems*
which he had translated into English. Karen introduced me
to Flannery O'Connor's brilliant short stories on which she
lectured and also on the poems of G. M. Hopkins, the English Jesuit.

My own lectures attempted to analyze Graham
Greene's *The Power and the Glory*, James Baldwin's *Go.
Tell it on the Mountain*, Elie Wiesel's *The Gates of the For-
est,* Albert Camus' *The Fall*, Ernest Hemingway's *The Old
Man and the Sea*, John Updike's *The Poorhouse Fair*, and
William Golding's *The Spire*. I also gave the comparative

lectures introducing the course and the concluding lecture. To read and reread these modern classics was to make this the most enjoyable course I have ever taught and I think it conveyed a sense of the beauty and relevance of religion to modern life without preaching at the students. No course for which I was primarily responsible has drawn greater numbers, beginning at about 65.

As the course developed we substituted other books such as Bernard Malamud's *The Fixer,* Frederick Buechner's *The Love Feast,* Dostoievsky's *The Brothers Karamazov,* Chaim Potok's *The Chosen*, Takeyama's *The Buddha Tree,* Paton's *Cry the Beloved Country*, Peter De Vries's *The Mackerel Plaza,* Charles William's *All Hallows Eve* and François Mauriac's *A Woman of the Pharisees.* We also used different books by some of the same authors, such as Wiesel's *Night,* Greene's *The Heart of the Matter,* and De Vries's *The Glory of the Hummingbird.* I can't resist citing two wisecracks in the last volume about the would-be author and henpecked husband as only an advertising man. This is his autobiographical poem:

> Through fol-de-rol and rigmarole
> This shall stand eternal,
> I'm the captain of my soul,
> But she's the lieutenant-colonel.

The second witticism is the proudest achievement of the advertiser celebrating the cereal as brainfood: "What's the thinking man's cereal? Joyce Carol Oates" (who is at present a professor of creative literature at Princeton university). How often have I quoted De Vries' Beatitude for the wildest car drivers: "Blessed are the pacemakers for they shall see God." This came from *The Mackerel Plaza.* the most brilliant satire on modern Liberal Protestantism and its desperate desire to be up-to-date. It might have been written as an essay on H. Richard Niebuhr's words: "A God without wrath brought men without sin into a kingdom without judgment through the ministrations of a Christ without a cross."

In later years my able associates in this course were Chava Weissler for the Jewish writers, Helen Hardacre (the successor of William LaFleur), who lectured on Japanese writers and my wife Marie-Hélène who had written a book on Buechner and who as a Parisienne, lectured on François Mauriac, Albert Camus, and André Gide. The essence of my lectures dealing with Christian authors were incorporated in a volume entitled, *Catching the Conscience: Essays in Religion and Literature* published by Cowley Publications of Cambridge, Massachusetts in 1984.

The other course that I taught was to a more restricted group, which varied from about 16 to 25 students in any given year. Its title was "Religious Images in Western Art". It was an introduction to the Judeo-Christian tradition by concentrating on its major phases of development as these were mirrored in art, architecture, theology and worship. The forms examined included Jewish, Byzantine, Romanesque, Protestant, Baroque and Modern. It began by considering Judaism and Christianity as forbidden faiths, insisting at the start on no graven images. It continued with the acceptance of images by tracing Hellenistic art and the symbols, in the Catacombs, and considering the controversial origins of the basilica. Byzantium came next, with the Emperor conceived as an earthly Christ leading to absolutism and its correctives and an account of the worship of the Eastern Orthodox Church. Our next concern was to consider the Church as both tamer and tutor in Romanesque and Gothic art and architecture, and their iconography, culminating in a study of the Mass as a medieval drama. After this came the Renaissance and the Reformation (the latter as a faith for the commonalty) with the representative artists: da Vinci and Michelangelo for the Renaissance and Dürer, Grunewald, and Rembrandt for Protestantism. Baroque Art was interpreted as that of the Catholic Church Militant, seen in the Council of Trent, the new Orders and Mystics that inspired Baroque, as reflected in El Greco, Zurbaran, and Caravaggio. Finally, we came to the twenti-

eth century, with Rouault, Epstein, Chagall, Picasso, Stanley Spencer and Abstract Expressionism, reflecting in one
way or another the new theological and ethical stresses
which emphasize horizontal rather than vertical relationships and conceive the Church or the Synagogue as God's
servant people. The Church criticizes war as fratricidal as
Picasso does in his *Guernica*, and sees sacrifice as essential
to religion (as in Sutherland's lower panel of his tapestry of
the Crucifixion in Coventry Cathedral) or in Rouault's
Head of Christ, and also senses the great need of joy in
contemporary life, as in the levitating lovers in the paintings of Chagall and in the dancing colors of the Vence
Chapel decorated by Henri Matisse.

I also spent a considerable time in administration. In
fact I was for a decade the Director of Graduate Studies of
the Department of Religion at Princeton from 1969 to 1979
under the chairmanships of Paul Ramsey, Philip Ashby and
R. B. Y. Scott. Here my task was to collect the application
forms of those who wished to be entrants to our Ph.D. program at Princeton University, evaluate them myself and
hand them to the colleagues who would be primarily responsible for teaching them, such as George Thomas, Malcolm Diamond and Victor Preller in the Philosophy of Religion; Arthur McGill in Theology; John Wilson and myself
in the history of Christianity; Paul Ramsey and Gene Outka
(later Jeffrey Stout) in Christian Ethics, and Philip Ashby
and Bill LaFleur (later Helen Hardacre) in the History of
Religions or Comparative Religion (as it is sometimes
called). It was also my responsibility to attend the monthly
meetings of the Directors of Graduate Studies of all Departments of the University, where we evaluated the new courses proposed by each Department of Study, along with other
common business introduced by the Dean of the Graduate
School of the University, Theodore Ziolkowski in my time.
Then I was also responsible for arranging the timing of the
General Examinations in the Department, collecting the
grades for the graduate courses in and outside the Department, and for arranging the times when the Final Examina-

tions leading to the M.A. degree would be held so that con-
flicts in dates were avoided. Also, I had to communicate
with the students engaged in writing their Ph.D. dissertations often outside the University to find out how they were
progressing and to determine the dates on which their Final
Public Oral would be held. My most important task was to
write recommendations for our graduates to vacant posts. A
lot of this work would seem to be dull in the extreme, but it
gave me great joy to get to know our students of whom we
admitted about eight each year and so our total was usually
about twenty or so in residence at any given time.

In the early years we were fortunate to receive a
substantial outside grant which we decided to use to invite
distinguished experts from other universities to lecture to
our graduate students. We then invited both faculty and
graduate students belonging to the sub-discipline of the lecturer to dine with him. This was a most civilized way of encouraging the exchanges proper to Academe.

I believe that my best work was the careful and ap-
preciative testimonials I would compose for our graduate
students, as well as the relaxing dinners we organized for
them. When the more rigorous faculty wanted to oust students who did not come up to our expectations without giving them a second chance, both George Thomas and I
pleaded for them. In the course of ten years, eighty to a
hundred passed through my hands. Most of them I remember, but naturally those I recall most vividly studied in
Church History and were taught by John Wilson and myself.

The most prolific of them was one of the five earliest graduate students in our program, John Everitt Booty,
now the official historiographer of the Episcopal Church,
who taught at the seminaries of that Church in Alexandria,
Virginia, and in Cambridge, Massachusetts, and became
Dean of the School of Theology at the university of the
South, Sewanee, Tennessee. His outstanding doctoral dissertation was published by the S.P.C.K. of London in 1963,
with the title of *John Jewel as Apologist of the Church of*

England. Professor Stephen Sykes, (later Bishop of Ely) in the festschrift devoted to him wrote that this was "A celebration of John Booty's combination of the virtues of the scholar and the mystic." This is evident in most of his works, such as *Three Anglican Divines on Prayer: Jewel, Andrewes and Hooker*, his edition of the first Edwardian Prayer Book, *The Book of Common Prayer, 1549* and of Jewel's *An Apology of the Church of England* (both of which were printed for the Folger Shakespeare Library by the University of Virginia.) He also contributed Volume IV of the important Folger Library Edition of the works of Richard Hooker published by the Harvard University Press, *Of the Laws of Ecclesiastical Polity: Attack and Response* (1976). His admiration for T. S. Eliot appeared in his book, *Meditating on the Four Quartets* (Cowley, 1983) and the latter publisher issued his *The Christ We Know* (1987) and *The Episcopal Church in Crisis* (1988). He and Stephen Sykes edited the important volume, *The Study of Anglicanism*, which the S.P.C.K. and Fortress Press in Philadelphia published in 1988. These are not all of his works. I am personally grateful to him for his editing of my festschrift in 1984, on my retirement from Princeton University, the title of which was, *The Divine Drama in History and Liturgy* (Allison Park, Pennsylvania: Pickwick Publications). I rejoice that he is relatively near in the summer to us in his retirement house in Center Sandwich, New Hampshire.

The early student who followed in my footsteps in publishing works on Puritanism is Dewey D. Wallace, Professor of Religion at George Washington University in Washington, D. C. One superb volume of his was *Puritans and Predestination: Grace in English Protestant Theology, 1525-1695*, published by the University of North Carolina Press in 1982. This was a profound, clear, and erudite volume. He had previously published a volume on *The Pilgrims* in the Consortium Series in 1977, and *The Spirituality of the later English Puritans: an anthology* issued by Mercer University Press in Macon, Georgia, appeared in

1987. At my retirement dinner he referred amusingly to my academic advice to him:

> Horton Davies suggested that I do my dissertation on John Owen. Little did I know that what that meant was reading the 24 volumes in fine print, of the works of John Owen, perhaps the most dreary of the 17th century theologians. But I persevered and even now on beautiful Spring days when I am in the Library [Folger] pondering many a quaint and curious volume of forgotten Puritan lore, I blame it and much of my misspent youth on Horton Davies.

Another early student, whose Ph. D. dissertation was published, and whose work followed my own liturgical interests was Julius W. Melton, for many years a development officer at Davidson College in North Carolina. It was titled *Presbyterian Worship in America: Changing Patterns since 1787,* published by the John Knox Press of Richmond, Virginia in 1967. It was a careful and illuminating study.

Another student of mine, who already had a Ph.D. in English, was W. D. White, whose dissertation was published as *The Preaching of John Henry Newman* by the Fortress Press of Philadelphia in 1969. It combined theological and literary analysis of Newman's superb English sermons with great insight.

The wittiest graduate student I ever had was too modest even to let me recommend his study of seventeenth century Anglican history to a publisher. He is Professor Howard Happ. Perhaps he was wise to devote himself to lecturing and administration rather than book-writing, because I know he had the dramatic flair of a lecturer who prepared to make history seem relevant by dressing up in an imitation of some of the leading personalities he lectured on.

It was only during my latter days that we began to get a few (and they were impressive) women graduate stu-

dents. One of them was Ellen Weaver, who, after teaching
in the Department of Religious Studies at Rutgers University in New Brunswick, New Jersey, went to Notre Dame
University in South Bend, Indiana, and endeared herself so
much that she became the Deputy Chairman of the Department of Theology. Her own theological insights were seen
in the impressive dissertation she wrote on the controversial
institution of Port-Royal, near Paris. Its full title is *The Evo-
lution of the Reform of Port-Royal from the Rule of Citeaux
to Jansenism* (1978). This work sheds light on the reason
for the supposition that Port-Royal's supporters seemed to
be moving in the direction of Calvinism because of its pre-
destinarian emphasis and its links with Pascal and his
friends, when in fact it was following the earlier, simpler
Biblical emphasis of its Cistercian foundation. It says much
for the book that it had a Parisian publisher, Beauchesne.

The second most prolific graduate student of mine
was Robert Alley, who dared to teach a liberal theology in
a relatively conservative institution, the Religion Department of the University of Richmond in Virginia, and afterwards was appointed with safer title, Professor of the Humanities. He has always shown the courage of his
convictions, and has always been a vigorous proponent of
religious liberty. It is not surprising, therefore, that he wrote
James Madison on Religious Liberty (Prometheus Books,
Buffalo, New York, 1985) or *So Help Me God: Religion
and the Presidency. Wilson to Nixon* (John Knox Press,
Richmond, 1972), or *The Supreme Court on Church and
State* (Oxford University Press, New York, 1988) which
dealt with cases involving freedom of religion. More surprising was his choice to write a book on the moral and ethical aspects of Television broadcasting, entitled, *Television:
Ethics for Hire?* (Abingdon Press, Nashville, 1977). In his
encomium at my retiral dinner, he thanked me for having
taught him about writing as well as thinking: "He taught me
quickly about my dissertation when after reading the first
chapter he said, 'Don't write it like it's a dissertation, write
it so that someone will want to read it.'" His subsequent

work shows how well he took the advice.

One of our brightest graduate students, William Seth Adams, now a professor at the Episcopal Seminary of the Southwest in Austin, Texas, wrote an admirable dissertation, as yet unpublished, on the historian of the High Church Anglican Oxford Movement of the nineteenth century. Its title was: "William Palmer of Worcester, 1803-1855: The Only Really learned Man among Them." This was in 1973. I well remember how he enjoyed his Final Public Oral Examination for the doctorate, in which after answering questions with relish and wit, he proceeded to pepper his examiners with his own questions.

Another outstanding graduate student was David Brown McIlhiney, a Harvard graduate in anthropology, whom I met when I was lecturing one summer at Union Theological Seminary in New York City, and who became a close friend. His doctoral dissertation was published as *A Gentleman in Every Slum: Church of England Missions in East London. 1837-1914* in 1988 by Pickwick Publications, Allison Park, Pennsylvania. It revised the general view that it was only High Church Anglicans that had worked in the slums of East London, showing that both Evangelicals and Broad Churchmen had also served there significantly. Because of his mother's illness he had to turn down an opportunity to become the first Chaplain of postgraduate students at Oxford University, which he had made his headquarters for his doctoral research. After a spell as Episcopal Chaplain at Dartmouth College in New Hampshire, he taught Religion as well as being Chaplain at Phillips Exeter School in Exeter, also in New Hampshire. He is now Rector of Trinity Episcopal Church in Claremont, New Hampshire, a community heavily hit by unemployment in the two recessions of this century. I shall never forget one joke that is told in his book of a Low Church lady who reported of a High Church Rector in East London that "he even practises celibacy openly in the streets"! Our encounter each summer in New England is a recurrent joy.

Another former graduate student and great friend is

Dr. Rogers Miles, whose progress in research was as lei-
surely as his culture was profound. His doctoral dissertation
took him ten years to complete, but the end product provides fascinating reading. This study of the Anglican Cler-
gy, entitled *Science, Religion and Belief: The Clerical Vir-
tuosi of the Royal Society of London, 1663-87,* is published
by Peter Lang. He is now professor of Religion at Whitman
College in the all too faraway state of Washington.

It is a source of great joy to me that so many of my
students have had their dissertations published, because that
is no common achievement, when one considers the thousands of unpublished doctoral dissertations, and the impetus of early publication as a means of academic promotion
and, ultimately, of gaining tenure.

It should be made clear that I have also taught many
other doctoral candidates in my seminars, but that the majority elected to write dissertations on American religious
history under the tutelage of my esteemed colleague, John
F. Wilson. It has also been my privilege to encourage outstanding undergraduates in the Department of Religion
with academic ambitions. I recall two in particular, both, of
whose fathers were physicians. The more recent graduate
was David Moessner who graduated from Princeton University with distinction, whose Senior Thesis on Martin Luther I directed, who later gained the top prize in Church
History at Princeton Theological Seminary, and went on to
take an Honors degree in Theology at my *alma mater*
Mansfield College in Oxford, studying New Testament under Professor George B. Caird, and finally took his D.
Theol. studying under Professor Markus Barth (a son of
Karl Barth). His first appointment was at Yale University
Divinity School and he then became a full professor at Columbia Theological Seminary in Decatur, Georgia. His first
and highly respected book is entitled, *Lord of the Banquet.
the literary and theological significance of the Lukan travel
narrative,* published in 1989 by the Fortress Press of Min-
neapolis. It is important because of the extraordinary emphasis made by St. Luke on the meals which Christ ate with

the marginal and the excluded, which liberation theologians in our time have rightly emphasized.

The other undergraduate with both literary and theological interests whom I also encouraged to study at Mansfield College, Oxford, is Professor Mason Lowance of the University of Massachusetts in Amherst, whose Ph.D. was obtained at Emory University, Atlanta, his home town. One of his books is a biography of the important American Puritan minister, who dominated the second generation of the New England population, *Increase Mather*. and this book was published by Twayne Publishers in 1974. This was followed six years later by his *magnum opus, The language of Canaan: metaphor and symbol in New England from the Puritans to the Transcendentalists*. This was published by the Harvard University Press in Cambridge, Massachusetts in 1980. It has both range and depth and literary astuteness in its historical exposition.

Only one of my students followed my complicated academic itinerary in three continents. That was Professor Victor J. Bredenkamp, who studied theology under me in Rhodes University, South Africa, went on to Mansfield College Oxford (while I taught there) and wisely concentrated on New Testament (not Church History) and finally came to study Old Testament for his Ph.D. at Princeton University under Professor R. B. Y. Scott. He is now the widely respected Professor of Divinity and Head of the Department at the University of Natal in Pietermaritzburg, South Africa.

The diversity of Princeton University students I have taught is best illustrated by two very different friends, Leon Hammond and David Cain. Leon was an entrepreneur who was cited regularly in Economics Courses in Princeton, for having established the selling of car tires from the early age of twelve . . . He took several of my courses and played the organ in the University Chapel for my wedding in 1973. He then worked for G.M., went to get an M.B.A. at Harvard and proceded to Yale to earn a Ph.D. in ethics. He is now married to a doctor and is a business administrator at Drew University.

David's Senior thesis was an exposition of a Dos-
toievski novel which he had turned into a drama which he
directed at the University Chapel. At Yale he and his wife
took a B.D. and he then returned to Princeton for his Doctorate in Theology under Arthur McGill. His passion for philosophical and existential theology is such that he reads
Kierkegaard in the original Danish and often travels to
Denmark. He is now a professor of religion at the Virginia
University campus at Fredericksburg.

Only two of my undergraduate students at Princeton
University are men of outstanding political distinction, and
both are Republicans. One is Senator John Danforth who
represents Missouri in the Senate of the United States and
is also a priest of the Episcopal Church, whom I taught in a
precept in my earlier days at Princeton. You can imagine
my delight when he turned up many years later in a class I
was teaching on Religion and Literature, sitting next to his
daughter and was instantly recognizable by the meche of
white that cuts across his dark hair. The other distinguished
politician I taught in an early course comparing English and
American History was until recently Governor Kean of
New Jersey, and I only recently learned that he was my student by chance. Attending a reception at the Governor's
Mansion in Princeton for faculty of Drew University
(where I taught for several years after my Princeton retirement), my wife and I moved forward in the queue to greet
him, and, after my name was read out, he put his arm round
me and said aloud: "My old teacher!"

As I look over these pages I am delighted that almost all of my students have remained in the academic pro-
fession and have made important contributions to knowledge in their books and articles. This has been a source of
encouragement to me and I am grateful for the warm response of both lively undergraduates and graduates.

10

FACULTY COLLEAGUES, FRIENDS, AND FAMILY

When you have taught at one institution, Princeton University, for 28 years, then your colleagues have become friends and are an extension of your family, so the categories in this chapter are happily confused.

FACULTY COLLEAGUES

Those I shall write about more fully have been my colleagues for the longest time, or members of my family. I begin with George F. Thomas because he was the Chairman of the Department when I was appointed and remained an advisor and close friend. A Rhodes Scholar at Queen's College, Oxford when the Reverend B. H. Streeter was the Provost or Head of the College, George respected the philosophical breadth and liberal attitude of this impressive man. Born in Texas in 1899, Dr. Thomas graduated from Southern Methodist University in 1919, from Oxford in 1923 with an Honours degree in Theology, and a Ph. D. in Philosophy from Harvard in 1929. He began as a teacher of English in a Texas High School, was an assistant professor of Religion for two years at Southern Methodist University, taught philosophy at Swarthmore College in Pennsylvania, which modelled its degrees on Oxford's curriculum and its degree examinations judged by external professors. He then taught philosophy as a full professor at Dartmouth College in Hanover, New Hampshire, from 1931 to 1937, and was most happily married in 1933 to Dorothy Boyd Graves, who taught the history of art at Mount Holyoke College and during four summers in the M.A. program at Middlebury College while George taught Philosophy of Religion. Her husband left Dartmouth to teach religion at the University of North Carolina at Chapel Hill, and in 1940 he came as Princeton's earliest Professor of Religion.

It was his program there in which the contribution of religion to culture was emphasized (rather than training for the ministry) that led to the creation of many imitations in the universities and colleges of the United States, and involved George in many visits and lectures on the new developments at Princeton. His regular lectures were marked by clarity and exemplary fairness even in discussing options that he did not favor, and all were given without a note so that he addressed his audience fully in their faces. His Chairmanship was marked by affection and careful consideration of all his colleagues. "Christian gentleman" is the term so often used of him and that seems to have fitted him best. On his retirement from Princeton he became the virtual founder of the Department of Religion in our sister University, Rutgers the State University of New Jersey, at their New Brunswick campus. And all the way through, his wife, Dorothy, our oldest Princeton friend, was his lively and lovely companion and a marvelous hostess to faculty and graduate students. I shall never forget the feasts and the carols we sang in their home with the graduate students every Christmas.

George's books were: *The Vitality of the Christian Tradition* (1944), which he edited, while he wrote *Poetry, Religion and the Spiritual Life* (1951), *Christian Ethics and Moral Philosophy* (1955), *Religious Philosophies of the West* (1965), and *Philosophy and Religious Belief* (1969). All were solid books, like their author. George Thomas was also a keen ecumenist as a member of the Advisory Commission of the World Council of Churches.

Our most productive colleague was the neo-orthodox theological ethicist, Paul Ramsey. A tall, broad man, with a Stentorian voice and hectoring manner (but all

in fun), he was born in Mendenhall, Mississippi, in 1913
and graduated from Millsaps College in the same State in
1935. He gained his B.D. at Yale Divinity School and his
Ph.D. at Yale University in 1943. He was awarded seven
Honorary doctorates in his lifetime, including two from
Catholic institutions and an Sc.D. from Worcester Poly-
technic Institute. He had a series of short term appointments at Millsaps College, and Garrett Biblical Institute in
Evanston, Illinois, until he joined the Princeton Religion faculty in 1944, where he remained until his retirement in
1982. He was a visiting member of faculty at different universities or colleges and his publication record was simply
staggering. Among his most influential books were *Basic
Christian Ethics* (1950), *Deeds and Rules in Christian Ethics* (1967), *The Just War: Force and Political Responsibility* (1968), *Fabricated Man: The Ethics of Genetic Control*
(1970), *The Patient as Person: Explorations of Medical
Ethics* (1971) and *Ethics at the Edges of Life: Medical and
Legal Intersections* (1978). He also edited Jonathan Edwards' *The Freedom of the Will* and *The Study of Religion
in Colleges and Universities* (1970). Like George Thomas
he became President of the American Theological Society.
Also, Paul was elected a member of the Institute of Medicine of the National Academy of Sciences (a rare honor!).

His last years were spent as a member of the newly
founded Center of Theological Inquiry in Princeton where
the Director informed me that he was the untitled Dean of
the institution. I was amused when he gave me the following single piece of advice: "Don't be so clear in your exposition: complexity is a better index of profundity!" What
astonished his colleagues was his combination of breadth
and depth, who also was invited by a major university such
as Yale to lecture to the faculties of medicine and law in
ethics. He was a brilliant man and, while I lacked his marvellous skills in rhetoric and debating, I shared his neo-
orthodox theology, believing like him that the Church was
too ready to sell out its revelation to appear relevant. I think
the favorite joke of his that I remember went as follows. It

concerned a brilliant candidate, thought to be an alcoholic, being interviewed for the headship of a private school by the Board of Trustees. One wily member suggested they put the candidate through a psychological association of ideas test. When the candidate appeared before them one trustee asked: "What do you think of when you hear the name Gordon?" The candidate replied: "The great Christian, General Gordon of Khartoum." The second trustee asked: "What do you think of when you hear the name Booth?" Without hesitation the candidate replied: " The Founder of the Salvation Army, of course." The third trustee asked: "What do you think of when you hear the term Vat 69?" The reply was equally rapid: "Isn't that the private telephone of His Holiness the Pope?" The upshot was they considered the candidate too intelligent for them, so they didn't appoint him. Paul Ramsey was not only a superb raconteur, but also a loyal friend.

The third colleague I worked most closely with was seventeen years younger than me, John Frederick Wilson, an outstanding administrator. We were the two church historians in the Department, which John joined in 1960, after graduating in history from Harvard University, and with M.Div. and Ph.D. degrees from Union Theological Seminary in New York City. He had been an assistant instructor and lecturer at Barnard College of Columbia University before coming to Princeton. While here, he was assistant Dean of the College for seven years, Chairman of the Department and Master of Forbes College the largest in the University. Somehow, (and this seems characteristic of his expertise) he managed recently in an economic downturn to obtain within a single year financial grants for research in Religion at Princeton from the Lilly and the Pew Foundations to the sum of $1,200,000! And this is the man whose ancestry goes back from Congregational minister to Congregational minister in a direct and unbroken line to the first teaching minister of the Boston church, John Wilson! He has, as one might guess, extraordinary consideration for his students at the undergraduate and graduate levels, and his wife, Ruth, has played an important part in Princeton's program for Teacher Preparation to enable future teachers to obtain teaching diplomas as well as their A.B. degrees in four years. John is presently the Director of a research project on Church and State. His first book was published by Princeton University Press and is a study of Cromwellian Puritanism, *Pulpit in Parliament* (1969). His other books are *Public Religion in American Culture* (1979), and *Church and State in American History* (1965, 1987) which he edited and to which he contributed. He also transcribed and edited the difficult manuscript of Jonathan Edwards' major work, *A History of the Work of Redemption* (1989). He was President of the American Society of Church History, and has had a host of admirable graduate students who did dissertations on American religious themes. In research projects he works happily with our Catholic historian, Professor Albert Raboteau, and with Professor Wuthnow of the Department of Sociology. It was his persuasiveness with the administration that enabled me to buy the present house in which we have lived since 1975 in an academic circle of Princeton, a real token of friendship. When I think of him I picture him with a very cautious and amused look, appropriate for a highly successful administrator and a critical scholar with high standards.

The most amusing and dramatic lecturer in the Department is Malcolm Luria Diamond who was here when I came. He has lectured to large undergraduate classes on Philosophy of Religion for all these years, while sharing his graduate responsibilities with Victor J. Preller, a high Anglican. Malcolm can expound Christianity as if he were a born Christian, but he also has the sense of social justice of the Jewish community. He graduated from Yale as a bachelor in engineering, spent a post-graduate year at Trinity College, Cambridge, and gained his Ph.D. in Columbia University in 1959. Soon after a year teaching at Sarah Lawrence College in Bronxville, New York, he joined the Princeton faculty in 1953 and retired in 1992 to devote himself full time to the private practice of psychological therapy. He was a successful therapist at Princeton's Corner

House for adolescent drug addicts from 1983 to 1987.

A man of wide and deep sympathy with added technical skill, he has a wide circle of friends, and his experience with the United States Naval Reserve from 1942 to 1945 has stood him in good stead in an easy approach to all types and conditions of folk. His high lecturing competence was acknowledged by the Harbison teaching award granted to him by the Danforth Foundation in 1970. His books include *Martin Buber: Jewish Existentialist* (1960), as well as *Contemporary Philosophy and Religious Thought* (1974), and he was co-editor of *The Logic of God* (1975). In 1978 he was appointed to the William H. Danforth Chair. The phrase "out of sight, out of mind" does not apply to him. When I underwent a moderately serious operation in recent years he visited me during recuperation. A trained man with unlimited compassion is bound to be a splendid therapist, which he has been to innumerable students in the advice he has given them.

Victor S. Preller has been Malcolm Diamond's colleague in the Philosophy of Religion for many years. He was both an undergraduate and a graduate student at Princeton University. He also gained a Bachelor of Sacred Theology degree at General Theological Seminary in New York City and is a priest of the Episcopal Church. He also did postgraduate studies at Munich University, where the leading theologian was Karl Rahner. In recent years he has been a greatly appreciated Master of the Graduate School. He is equally at home in Philosophy of Religion and Systematic Theology, and he proved his high competence in both disciplines in his profound work, *Divine Science and the Science of God: A Reformulation of Thomas Aquinas* (1967) published by the Princeton University Press. He is a thoughtful man and a helpful advisor.

Colleagues with whom I have worked more recently include John Gager and Jeffrey Stout. Professor Gager graduated from Yale with an A.B. in French, having spent a year at the Sorbonne, and gained his B.D. from Yale and his Ph.D. from Harvard, and spent a year studying in

Tübingen University. His first academic appointment was at Haverford College in Pennsylvania, and his specialty is teaching and researching early Christianity and Judaism in the first few centuries of the Common Era, as the titles of his books indicate. He has published *Moses in Graeco-Roman Paganism* (1972), *Kingdom and Community: the social world of early Christianity* (1975), and *The origins of anti-semitism: attitudes towards Judaism in pagan and Christian antiquity* (1983). He has twice been Chairman of the Department and was a most useful advisor to me during my year in the chair. A very friendly and vivacious lecturer and conversationalist, he is deservedly popular. He has succeeded John Wilson as Master of Forbes College.

Jeffrey Stout is an authority on Religious Ethics who joined our Department in 1975, and gained tenure in 1983. He graduated with an A.B. *magna cum laude* from Brown University in 1972, and gained his Ph.D. from Princeton University in 1976. He has published two volumes with striking titles: *The Flight from Authority: religion, morality, and the quest for autonomy* (University of Notre Dame Press, 1981), and *Ethics after Babel: the languages of morals and their discontents* (Beacon Press, 1988). He is the Department's most able technocrat for he made ours the first Department in the University to instruct our undergraduate majors in the use of computers for research papers, directing an IBM grant for this purpose. He is an impressive teacher, editor and administrator. In 1992 he became Chairman of the Department.

Other colleagues in the Department during my years of teaching there have been Helen Hardacre, Martha Himmelfarb and Elaine Pagels. Helen Hardacre has had a brilliant career. She did her doctorate in the History of Religions at Chicago University, concentrating on Japanese Religions, and I was happy to have her expertise in my course in "Religion and Literature". Her fame spread early from a series of very learned books appearing in quick succession from major university presses. These were: *Lay Buddhism in Contemporary Japan* (1984), *Kurozmikvo and the New Religions of Japan* (1986), *The Religion of Japan's Korean Minority* (1984), and, co-edited with Alan Sponberg, also of our Department, *Maitreye. The Future Buddha* (1987). She left us to head an Institute for the study of religions in Australia and in 1992 returned to this country to become a professor at Harvard University.

Martha Himmelfarb has produced four children and one book so far. Its intriguing title is *Tours of Hell: An Apocalyptic Form in Jewish and Christian Literature*. She has taught at Princeton since 1978 and now has a tenured post. Her husband is a sculptor of distinction. She is a happy, able, quiet, and contented lady. She graduated with an A.B. in Greek from Barnard College, and with a Ph.D. from the University of Pennsylvania, and was rightly delighted that the same university published her first book. She is now the effective Director of the graduate students and studies in the Department

I was a colleague for only two years with two outstanding teachers and scholars. One was Elaine Pagels, a historian who is an expert in the study of heretics in the first few Christian centuries. Her A.B. was gained in Stanford University and her Ph.D. from Harvard in 1970. She taught the history of religion at Barnard College, Columbia from 1970 to 1982 and was Chairman of the Department. She has been awarded research grants by six different foundations, including the most prestigious of all: she was a MacArthur Prize Fellow from 1981 to 1987. She has, as might be expected, a notable publication record. This includes *The Johannine Gospel in gnostic exegesis* (1973), *The gnostic Paul: gnostic exegesis of the Pauline letters* (1975), *The gnostic Gospels* (1979), *and Adam, Eve and the Serpent* (1988) as well as commentaries on the Nag Hammadi Codices in 1984 and 1990. She has also known the bitterness of tragedy in the death of a young child and, in July 1988, in the death of her husband, Heinz Rudolph Pagels, a theoretical physicist, from a fall while mountainclimbing in Colorado. She is an attractive, brilliant, and courageous lady. She was recently elected to the American

Academy of Arts and Sciences.

The other person who was also my colleague for only two years is Albert Raboteau, who gained his B.A. from Loyola-Marymount College in English, his M.A. also in English from the University of California at Berkeley, and his Ph.D. in Religious Studies from Yale University. This brilliant African-American was assistant professor at Yale (1973-75), Associate Professor at Berkeley (1979-82) where he was also a Dean, and he joined the Princeton faculty in 1982. He, too, has gained several research awards. His two books are: *Slave Religion: the "invisible institution" in the Ante-Bellum South,* published by Oxford University Press of New York in 1978, and *Religion and the slave family in the Antebellum South* which Notre Dame University Press brought out in 1980. He has been Chairman of our Department of Religion. He is a man of great warmth, as well as of scholastic and administrative ability. In 1992 he was appointed Dean of Princeton's Graduate School.

My closest friend on the faculty of the Department, partly through our closeness of age, but also through sheer compatibility, was Philip Harrison Ashby, our first historian of religions, who was an expert in the religions of India. His doctorate came from the University of Chicago. It is to him alone that I owe my dangerous delight in drinking gin martinis, which I curb by restricting the consumption of them to once a week on Fridays only. Otherwise I have to be satisfied with Scotch or wine, both anticlimactic in my comparisons. Philip's books were *The Conflict of Religions* (Scribner's 1955), *The History and Future of Religious Thought* (1963), *Modern Trends in Hinduisim* (Columbia University Press, 1974), and *Reflections of a Historian of Religion* (Whitworth College Spokane, 1984). I have missed him deeply since he took early retirement and went to live on Rockway Beach, Bainbridge Island in the far off State of Washington in a house built with his own hands. He'll be amused that I never see a Buick car without thinking of him because he worked his way through college sell-

ing Buicks! He, too, like John Wilson, was an Assistant
Dean at Princeton University and he chaired the Department from 1968 to 1973. He was a generous, affectionate,
and devoted friend, and his wife Kelley was a gifted hostess.

It is clear that we have been extraordinarily fortunate in the faculty we have been able to attract to the Department of Religion at Princeton University. Not to make
this chapter more ponderous, I have to omit appreciation of
two professors of New Testament, W. D. Davies and
Franklin W. Young, who both went to Duke. The latter was
also chairman of the department, and remains a friend. Two
ethicists Gene Outka and John P. Reeder left respectively
for chairs at Yale and at Brown Universities. Arthur
McGill, our theologian, left us for Harvard Divinity School.
From my knowledge of my colleagues, they have been singularly free from one academic vice, namely that of envy.
We have all been delighted to share the joy of the many
achievements of other members of the faculty.

OTHER FRIENDS

As I remember faculty members who have been
friends to me in the dim and distant past, two spring to
mind from my days in Europe, and two from my South African days, and one from outside Princeton in the United
States. My first teacher of systematic theology in Yorkshire
United Independent College, Bradford, England, was an
Australian, Hubert Cunliffe-Jones, who later became the
first Professor of Theology in Manchester University. He
communicated a love in me for historical theology, which
began by an enthusiastic introduction to Saint Augustine of
Hippo, requiring me to read his *Confessions* and his *City of
God,* and then he introduced me to another masterpiece, *On
the Incarnation* of Saint Athanasius. I owe to him the ambi-
tion to become a church historian. He, it was, who later
helped me to enter his own English theological college,

Mansfield College, Oxford. Here I admired the learned and witty Principal, Dr. Nathaniel Micklem, though I was too much in awe of him for him to be a friend. I admired his remarkable wit and his enthusiastic ecumenical outlook.

In my students days there I was much closer to Chaplain John Marsh, like myself, an Edinburgh graduate, who obtained a first class honours in Philosophy and was a favorite student of the distinguished Professor of Moral Philosophy there, Dr. A. E. Taylor. John was a genuine friend to every student, who went hiking with them in the Lake District in the vacations, and encouraged them as they rode in the St. Catherine's boat on the river Isis. The same qualities were retained (with the addition of a little decorum) when he later left his chair in the University of Nottingham to become Principal of Mansfield, when he invited me to join his faculty. It was clearly a disappointment to him that I left after only two years, but in later years he invited me back to teach at the Mansfield Summer School. If occasionally irate, he was expert in the art of forgiveness.

My two friends in South Africa were Leslie A. Hewson and James Irving, the former a great Christian and the latter an atheist but a keen proponent of social justice as a Communist—the kindest I have ever met. Leslie Hewson was a Methodist minister and for many years the Warden of Livingstone House, the Hostel for all non-Anglican theological students at Rhodes University, where they were taught practical theology such as how to preach, conduct worship, and visit church members at home or in hospital. I admired Leslie so much that when he was elected President of the Methodist Church of South Africa, I wrote to *The Christian Recorder*, the leading English-medium religious newspaper, asking them to print my encomium of him. In that testimonial I wrote: "He is a genuine Swan. I think the image of a swan is suitable, for it is characterised by gracefulness (and I do not know a more courteous man), the whiteness of integrity (he is a most honorable man), and a sure, straight course (loyal to Scriptural holiness both as a good Methodist and a good New Testament scholar), who obtained first class Honours in the Theological Tripos in the B.A. degree of Cambridge University." Although invited to a full professorship in another university he remained in the lowlier office of Warden, until Rhodes eventually gave him the professorship of New Testament Studies he richly deserved. My other friend in Grahamstown, Professor of Sociology James Irving, I have spoken of warmly earlier, but I do not think I indicated that it was his rough upbringing in the poverty of Glasgow that inclined him to extreme Socialism, and that it was only as an older student that he gained his first class honours degree in Social Anthropology at Cambridge University, the financing of which was made possible by political supporters. We had many discussions, but religion was for him taboo, for *me* life.

I did not live close enough to him for long enough for me to be able to call this Benedictine monk, Father Godfrey Dickmann, O.S. B., a great friend, but he was certainly much more than an acquaintance. Readers of this book will know that worship is for me (as for all Benedictines) the central act of the Christian life, the *opus Dei*, as St. Benedict called it (the work of God). I came to know Father Godfrey through his closeness to Protestant observers at the great Roman Catholic Council known as Vatican II, where Father Godfrey was a *peritus* (or expert) in worship. He and the World Chairman of Quakerism, Dr. Douglas Steere, a Protestant observer at Vatican II, determined to express their ecumenical convictions by gathering a group of Catholics and Protestants who were convinced that spirituality can cross denominational frontiers.

This group to which I belonged used to meet once annually alternately at a Catholic monastery or abbey or at a Protestant retreat center or theological seminary to share worship and talk about our different traditions. We even produced a book edited by Michael Marx, also a Benedictine, called *Protestants and Catholics on the Spiritual Life,* published by the Liturgical Press, Collegeville, Minnesota in 1965. It was through his interest that I became a founding trustee of the Ecumenical Institute at St. John's Abbey and gave lectures on Anglican and Protestant Liturgics there during two summers, most recently in 1979 when my wife Marie-Hélène delighted the monastic audience with her lectures on Catholic novelists like Mauriac and Greene, and Flannery O'Connor. These were opportunities to renew our friendship with Father Godfrey and to go gathering mushrooms with him. He was a top theological liturgiologist in North America, and his enthusiasm for worship, for the vernacular, for the desirability of ordaining women priests, and for anecdotal stories, was unquenchable.

I am able to repeat two of these stories because they are recorded in Kathleen Hughes' stimulating biography of Godfrey, entitled *The Monk's Tale* (Liturgical Press, Collegeville, 1991). At Vatican II, Godfrey reported that as several Council Fathers couldn't understand Italian, green and red lights flashed near the rest rooms the words "*sede vacante*" and "*gloriose regnante*" ("Vacant See" and "Gloriously reigning" used to describe a Diocese either without or with the resident occupant of the See!) Godfrey also reported a bishop criticizing the dominance of the Curia in the Council as saying, "They are giving us the mushroom treatment: Keep 'em in the dark and feed 'em horse manure." As a fungophile Godfrey loved that particular joke. A more joyful man I have never encountered.

AND FAMILY

In this section of the chapter I shall refer to my brothers, Dorian and Michael, my sister Gloria, and my daughter and two sons, Christine, Hugh, and Philip, while merely listing the names of my grandchildren who have yet to develop their potential.

Dorian, my younger brother, was an engineer officer in the Merchant Navy in World War II. In fact, I am very proud of his achievements. In 1987 he retired as chief executive officer of James Walker and Company with its headquarters in Working, Surrey, England. It has the most attractive Board Room I have ever seen because in Victorian days it housed the Royal Dramatic College and was its Central Hall. It is decorated with circular windows of stained glass representing scenes from the Comedies and Tragedies of Shakespeare. Later these buildings became an Oriental Institute and close to the Institute was built a mosque which still stands among the many buildings that house the firm.

Dorian's responsibilities can be measured by the fact that the firm which fabricates seals of many materials to prevent the loss of steam, gas, oil, or other contents in machinery in a multitude of applications, has seven factories and twenty-seven depots in the United Kingdom. It also has twenty-seven wholly owned subsidary companies overseas, including 6 in Australia, 5 in France, 3 each in Belgium, Holland and Italy, 2 each in Eire, New Zealand and Spain and 1 in Glenwood, Illinois, U.S.A. The total number of employees in 1982, its hundredth year of operation, was over 2,600. Moreover, the firm's technology in sealing liquids gained technical and exportation success. The materials had to meet hitherto inexperienced pressure when employed in communication satellites, in airplanes, in petro-chemical factories, as well as in gas and oil exploration, and also in ocean liners, warship and huge oil-tankers.

The quality of the design and the varied applications of the technology were proven to be the highest quality by the awards the Company received. In 1972 it gained the Queen's Award in Industry for excellence in design manufacture, technology, and export achievement. In addition, a subsidiary company such as Rotobolt Limited gained the Queen's Award for Technical Achievement and the Duke of Edinburgh's Award for Design, both in 1985.

To have headed this vast group of factories, agencies, and depots was an immense responsibility. It must have given Dorian great pleasure that in recognition of his splendid leadership the Board of Directors insisted that his portrait was to be painted by the artist who was chosen to depict the Queen of England. This portrait now hangs in the Board Room. It was always a delight for me that when Dorian visited the American factory every two years he also spent a long weekend with us in our summer house in Vermont, occasionally accompanied by Joan, his wife. She loves the outdoor sport of bowling, solves the intricate cross-word puzzles of the London *Times*. and is a regular correspondent. They have three daughters and several grandchildren living nearby.

My half-sister, Gloria Scott and her husband Michael, have led a fascinating life, since she is both a trained nurse and schoolteacher, while he is an expert and experienced management consultant. When at home, which is rare, they live in an elegant eighteenth century house in Merstham, Surrey. Michael has served for twelve years in the United Nations in its Technical Cooperation Programme in Romania, Iraq, Sri Lanka, and Tanzania. Subsequently he has been under the aegis of the British Service Overseas where he has served for shorter periods twice in the Seychelles and also in the Cayman Islands. He has obviously been greatly appreciated for his expert technical and also psychological advice in management, and his wife has been an admirable helper and hostess. Like myself Michael has taken up painting in his retirement. .

My half brother Michael Davies is most amiable. He was born in Southampton, lived for many years in the Isle of Jersey where he was the Assistant Superintendent of the Island's Electricity Plant. He now lives in an exquisite thatched cottage on the Devon-Dorset border near Lyme Regis. Until recently he kept a small farm there. He hopes to sell part of the land on which the cottage lies and to spend the winters in Portugal where the idea of farming cork trees appeals to him. Michael's farming task was made the harder because of a hip iniury inflicted when his motorbike was hit by a careless car driver. Liz, his hard-working wife, is a great help to him, and welcomes us on the rare occasions when we can visit them.

The closest part of our family comprises three children: Christine, who was born in Croydon, England, in 1945, Hugh, born in Grahamstown, South Africa, in 1948, and Philip, born in Oxford, England, in 1955. Christine has inherited her mother Brenda's love and competence in music, and our joint love for the Church. She attended Smith College in Northampton, Massachusetts, where she gained her degree with Religion as her major. She was a good mother and kind step-mother to four boys in two successive marriages of whom Ricky and Jesse are my two grandsons. Her faith and her friends in the Church at Irvington-on-Hudson and beyond that have kept her going. I admire both her warmth and her unusual courage.

Our two boys followed their father in their dominantly visual esthetic passions. Hugh has had a stellar career as an Art Director. At Princeton University he graduated in the Art and Archaeology Department with a Bachelor of Arts degree *summa cum laude* (with the highest honors), followed by an M.F.A. and a Ph.D. In subsequent years he has directed the American exhibit at the Venice Biennale, been founding director of the Art Museum of the University of Massachusetts at Amherst, and Director of the Museum of Contemporary Art of San Diego in its original campus in lovely La Jolla (from which you can see sea lions swimming) and which is to be extended by the architect Robert Venturi. He has recently opened a satellite gallery in central downtown San Diego. While his standards are high in art, he is also a man of compassion and is eager to show the works of outstanding contemporary Mexican artists from over the border. It was a pleasure to co-author a volume with him, *Sacred art in a Secular Century,* melding our two areas of expertise. His second wife, Lynda, is the Senior Curator of the La Jolla Museum, and her daughter Mckenzie and his daughter, Alexandra are great friends, and help to tend young Dorian.

My younger son, Philip, is an outstanding photographer. He had only to present his portfolio and he was awarded a six year scholarship at the Massachusetts Art Institute, the only federally supported art institution from its foundation. He has worked as an assistant to a commercial photographer, but he became bored with the task of picturing mothers and babies and such routine requirements. So he now concentrates on wedding photographs and supplements his income by taxi-driving, which especially at nights in a large city like Boston can be a dangerous occupation. His wife Carol Hager, is also a Bachelor of Arts of the same institution and earns her living as a graphic designer. She is as calm as Philip is enthusiastic. He is the tall, handsome member of our family, just over 6 feet two inches in height. Since Boston is relatively near to Vermont we see them at least once a year in the summer. The originality of Philip as photographer is seen in his search for beauty in what others might term ugliness. He finds his subjects in run down, empty factories and industrial scenes of waste. This, and writing poetry, are among his chief delights.

My chief joy is my second wife, Marie-Hélène. I appreciate her doctoral degree at the Sorbonne, her three books, and her beauty of face and character, and her intelligence and sensitivity. I also admire my former wife, Brenda, who became a deeply valued life elder at the Nassau Presbyterian Church in Princeton and is Treasurer for the Women's Association of the entire Presbytery. Brenda lives in adjacent Kingston which is convenient for the visits of our three children. Her great pleasure is in playing the recorder.

11

ACTIVE RETIREMENT

No active person contemplates his retirement without some degree of anxiety, and I was no exception. But there were five compensations which prepared me for a happy and active retirement. The first of these was the retirement dinner itself in May of 1984 in which friends and family cheered me by their heartfelt expressions of gratitude, and the fact that some had come at their own charges from great distances to be there.

The second compensation was that I had planned to take an educational tour of the fabled land of Israel, where I hoped to visualise the scenes of so many important Biblical events, and also acquaint myself with the heroic attempt of the Jews to create a refuge for the persecuted from many lands. This would take place late in the Fall of 1984.

The third factor assisting my retirement was the fact that three academic institutions proposed to use my services. I would continue to teach each alternate year at Princeton Theological Seminary until 1988. Also Drew University Graduate School and Theological Seminary, where I had been teaching in the new Ph.D. program in Liturgics since 1978, invited me to continue as long as my health permitted by directing an annual Graduate Seminar on worship. This responsibility has lasted for over 15 years.

I was also invited to research at the new Center of Theological Inquiry at Princeton, from 1987 to 1991, with half a year off in 1990 because my wife had won the research award for secondary school teachers of New Jersey granted by the National Endowment of the Humanities, and was to write research articles about Molière. We also took all the summers off in Vermont, so that I hardly stretched the permitted maximum of three years allowed to a single researcher.

The next factor—a most important psychological consideration—was that I could devote myself to painting, my cherished avocation. Lastly, I had at last time to devote to social work in Habitat-for-Humanity.

The retirement dinner which my historian colleague, John Wilson, had planned was most cheering. Invitations went out to over a hundred people, including my family, my colleagues, and several of my graduate students. A festschrift was prepared by John E. Booty, my first graduate student, to which several of those present had contributed, including my son Hugh. My photograph was provided by my son Philip, the chronology of the major events of my life prepared by daughter Christine, and the extensive bibliography of my books and articles was the work of my wife, Marie Hélène, who gave a talk which ironically imitated my style of writing. The spirit of the evening was festive, jocular, and exuberant.

It was marked by many speeches and three presentations. First, John Booty presented me with a copy of the festschrift, *The Divine Drama in History and Liturgy* in the presence of the publisher, Dikran Y. Hadidian and his wife, Jean, our close friends, whose imprint is Pickwick Publications, Allison Park, Pennsylvania. Then there was the presentation of a portrait of me painted in oils by my friend from South African days, Dr. Gordon Wiles who had been Chairman of the Department of Religion at Connecticut College in New London before his retirement. In his speech he said that this portrait reminded him of the little boy who went to the zoo and got too near the lion who ate him, and when his mother was informed, she replied: "I'm vexed and him in his Sunday suit, too." In my case the vermilion and grey D.Litt. gown of Oxford looked more like a Christmas suit! I deeply appreciated the expertise and kindness this gift expressed. The third presentation was made by the incoming Chairman of the Department, John Gager, who in offering me a Princeton University Chair asked me to accept it as a gift from my colleagues, because retirement means giving up one's chair "so that you don't need to be left standing in the years to come."

The evening was one of great fun and my former students enjoyed roasting and toasting me. I shall select the more amusing parts of the speeches. Dr. James McCord, the recently retired President of Princeton Theological Seminary, where I had lectured for many years on Liturgics, referred to my being a Welshman, adding this joke. "He comes from Great Britain. It is a small island inhabited by four very quaint races. They're the English, a race of self-made people who worship their maker, and the Scotch who keep the Ten Commandments and everything else they lay their hands on. The Irish who fight all the time and don't have a ghost of an idea why they are fighting, and the Welsh, who pray on their knees on Sunday and prey on their neighbors the other six days of the week."

A former graduate student, Dr. Julius Melton, amused us by describing the possible ways of inventing a retirement service from the Bible, including the use of such accessories as tent pegs, daggers, stones of various sizes, and various wild beasts. Most retirements were clearly thanatalogical! Those in the early Church who avoided vulnerability by venerability apparently were placed by their friends on a pillar like St. Simeon Stylites. He observed that I had anticipated retirement beautifully: "Horton has been persuaded by more foundations and awarders of prizes to stay away from his job than anyone I know." Like other speakers he referred to my exotic tastes in cars and odd pronunciation of the word "Jaguar".

Dr. Howard Happ, came all the way from Southern California and recalling my interest for the unusual groups in left-wing Puritanism in seventeenth century England, pretended that he was bringing the greetings of the Muggletonians, a curious group that really flourished for a brief time. He pretended that a survivor had written a poem honoring me now translated from medieval Welsh. This is how it went:

> Once to every man of station comes the moment to retire,
> Thus set free for full creation while he still has life and
> fire;
> Not time's slave is Horton Davies, full of vigor, free from
> strife,
> As he reaches elevation in the liturgy of life.
> Shall we praise him for the labors of his mind, his pen, his
> desk,
> Or for teaching us the savors of Baroque and Romanesque?
> Will he be sainted for what he's painted, or for his insights
> into art?
> Or for the fond and friendly feelings from his Welsh and
> winsome heart?
> Does he wonder if he dare go on to perfect each dazzling
> gift,
> As we sing his *tantum ergo* and subscribe to his fest-
> schrift?
> Let him take deserved leisure,
> Roam the world, museums, or as he basks in peace and
> pleasure,
> To each trophy he'll add more.

Rodney Sawatksky also came from afar, Canada, and conjectured he'd been invited as a fellow member of the British empire with myself. Hence he alleged that "knowing this evening wouldn't be opened and concluded properly, actually Horton and I snuck off to the men's washroom just before the evening and we sang 'God save the Queen' together."

Another old friend, whom I taught as an undergraduate, Leon Hammond, joked about my moderately left-wing political views, calling me "a closet-capitalist" and asserted in proof that I was advised by him to buy a Chevrolet Citation, since that car possessed "a modicum of social realism," but, to his horror, I bought a Cadillac. Others laughed at its "powder blue" color.

The most amusing speech of all was that of Emeritus Professor, Paul Ramsey. He remarked on my obvious dislike of the office of Chairman of the Department in my last year.

> From my perch in Seventy-Nine Hall I observed that you, suffering from the chairmanship of the department thrust on you for one year before retirement, have carried out the responsibilities of that office with the aplomb of the man Lincoln told about, who being ridden out of town on a rail said he preferred not but for the honor of the thing. He'd come to the office in the early morning so that everyone sees you there, busy, busy, busy. Then go to your study at home where you'd rather be, returning at appointed times later in the day. That way Gwen the dog gets more exercise and I am told some socialization.

Later he referred to the deterioration of the Departmental courses when religion in general replaced specific religions. Hence, he prophesied, "You and I may expect courses instead of being titled "Reformation and Counter-Reformation" to be entitled rather, "Religion in the North-East Quadrant of the Eurasian Continent" or find a course on the Protestant Reformation titled as "The Silent Grief of Katherine Von Bora during Luther's table talk."

On a more serious note, John Wilson closed by referring to our collaboration in the Department, my attempts to help him in his own research into English Puritanism, and how I set a good example of an academic advisor. All this, however, was countered with quips about the private Horton, who liked risque limericks, and had an odd choice of cars. He claimed that the Dean of Students who was a colleague in the Department, Eugene Lowe, had investigated the type of cars driven by faculty members, and that there were only three Cadillacs in the university, and only one was colored powder blue. Nor did he forget the maroon and black Jaguar I once owned.

In my own speech I tried to retain the jocular spirit

of the evening. I began by telling the story of the 19th century English satirical poet, C. S. Calverley, who was expelled from both of the ancient English universities. When he came to Oxford he had to undergo a dull, conventional examination on the Anglican 39 Articles (of Faith). The black-gowned clerical dons asked him: "Mister Calverley, what is your attitude towards the Decalogue?" And he, in trying to hide his ignorance, replied: "Gentlemen, I have feelings of gratitude, not unmingled with awe and admiration." That, I claimed, was exactly my feeling at that time. Gratitude for all who came, gratitude for those who planned the event, and gratitude to have worked so happily with John Wilson for all those years. I thanked my old friend Gordon Wiles for his portrait of many colors, but said it would be more appropriate to have had me whitewashed. I recalled the lady who came to be photographed and disliked her photograph, saying: "you didn't do me justice." The photographer replied: "What you need, ma'am, is not justice but mercy." I thanked Gordon Wiles for the mercy he'd shown in depicting my ageing body. I ended by the reminder that Reinhold Niebuhr had said that forgiveness is the crown of Christian ethics. I thought a double forgiveness was necessary this evening, "once for all the kind lies that you told about me, and, twice, that I loved it!" With such gratitude I was well prepared for retirement from Princeton University after teaching in it for 28 years.

PILGRIMAGE TO ISRAEL

The second compensating factor was that I could also make the pilgrimage to Israel which I had promised myself for so many years. From November 5th to 15th, 1984, I was part of a travelling group of ministers and wives. This was planned in detail by two ladies from Livingstone, New Jersey, Mrs. Cecil Shar and her daughter, Mrs. Marilyn Ziemke, who also accompanied us. Their tours were organized as learning experiences, and for the two ladies was a way of commemorating a beloved daughter and sister. We spent five days in Jerusalem, two in Tiberias overlooking the Sea of Galilee, and two at Tel Aviv, in each case at Hilton Hotels, so we were not roughing it. The tour concentrated on Judea and Galilee.

We ascended the mountain peaks of Biblical history: Mount Zion, the Mount of Olives, the Mount of the Beatitudes, Mount Scopus, and the Golan Heights. The chief towns we visited (in addition to those previously mentioned) were Bethlehem, Nazareth, Bethany, Capernaum, and Emmaus sacred to the Christian saga, and also Jericho. We stopped for devotional moments at the Garden of Gethsemane where the 2000 years old olive trees were as contorted as Jesus there praying "Take this cup away from me," and we walked along the *Via Dolorosa* to the site of the Crucifixion, stopping at the place where the soldiers mocked Christ as a King, and went to the presumed locus of the Garden Tomb. The world too was very much with us, since we were passing by shops where the Muslim boys pestered us with their wares, pushing them in our faces and crying "dolláre" "dolláre."

We were also eager to share the exciting modern Jewish experience and achievements as reflected in the Israel Museum and in the memorial of the Holocaust in Yad Vashem, and to see the Knesset (the parliament building) made glorious by the paintings of the Russian Jew, Marc Chagall. We also visited the Western (Wailing) Wall of Jerusalem on the Friday evening sabbath at its commencement. We had an appropriately simple lunch at the Jewish kibbutz, Ayelet Hashahar, (The Morning Star) where we learned of the remarkable cooperation, self-discipline and sharing that makes such experiments in social living succeed.

We also visited a Christian Cooperative called Ness Ammin (A sign to the Nations), which was founded by Dr. Johan Pilon, a medical Missionary of the Church of Scotland. Its aim is not to convert Jews into Christians, but to witness to the need for cooperation with them at the deepest level. It bore the symbol of a fish (because the letters of the

Greek word for a fish spell the first letters of the words of a brief creed: Jesus Christ Son of God Savior) together with an olive branch to symbolize the turning over of a new leaf in the relations between Christians and Jews. We also visited the largest campus of the Hebrew University in Jerusalem. The University as a whole in several locations has over 16,000 students full-time and over 2,000 faculty members. Believing in the importance of first things first, they have many lecture rooms, libraries, laboratories, and dormitories, but no swimming pools or tennis courts when we were there. We also visited the Dead Sea, and saw the hole in the mountainside where a goatherd found the Dead Sea Scrolls, and viewed the settlement of the Essenes at Qumran.

There was far too much to summarize in a few pages, but I must first provide a general impression of Israel as a whole, and then emphasize three experiences, one Christian, one Jewish, and the third simply amusing.

In general, I was amazed by the smallness of Israel (only half the area of New Jersey), and its few natural advantages, with so much desert and wilderness, surrounded by 23 Arab and dominantly hostile nations, lacking gold and diamonds and its oil potential not fully determined as yet, and its eight months of the year without rain. Yet despite these dismal disadvantages this new country with deep historical roots, had made its desert blossom with orchards, grain, and flowers, and was defending itself with an army in which each citizen spends two years, and has made a home for immigrants from 73 countries since 1947. One is simply astonished by the courage, determination, brilliance theoretical and practical, the social experiments of the kibbutzim, and the musical and artistic genius of the Jewish people, and how important their land has been for the three monotheistic faiths, Judaism, Christianity, and Islam, whose relationships should be cooperative rather than conflicting.

Now I will mention the three experiences. The major Christian experience for me was to visit the Garden Tomb of Jesus in Gethsemane, which was bought a century ago through the influence of Gordon of Khartoum. I was convinced that this was very probably the site of the grave of our Lord (rather than the Church of the Entombment) and for four main reasons. Its shape, to begin with, seemed right, with an elevation in the tomb for the head and a lower part for the body. This paralleled the Gospel account of how John and Peter found the headcloth and the shroud. Archaeologically, it is first-century Herodian. In the third place, Joseph of Arimathea could easily have had his tomb in a commercial garden area nearby. Also, near this was discovered a winepress and not more than 80 yards away the hill of skulls that even today suggests a skull in the rock. Finally, the very location of the Garden Tomb close to a public highway and beside the North Wall of Jerusalem was highly appropriate as a warning issued by the Romans to potential political rebels. I found it not only convincing, but most moving to reflect that here the women followers of Christ met the death of death in Him and were filled with hope, like countless millions of Christians after them, through His Resurrection.

My most moving Jewish experience was at Yad Vashem, the Holocaust Museum where, in a ghastly and ghostly half-light one could make out the carved names of the places where six million Jews were murdered by the Nazis in World War in 21 places in Poland and Germany such as Auschwitz and Belsen. Most impressive to me was the outdoor sculpture of Nandor Glid, with its many thin arms, legs and bodies, looking like a human barbed-wire fence, with flesh instead of barbed wire, pleading so eloquently and pitiably for the mercy denied them. This I recall more vividly than the beautiful Dome of the Rock where Abraham was ready to sacrifice his son.

My amusing experience was the visit to the Dead Sea. We stopped at a bathing place where we floated on the heavily salted sea and swam for a short time. Then in order to remove the salt from our bodies we cold-showered on the beach. Then we went into a hot sulphur bath. This was immensely relaxing, but a notice informed us that we were not to stay in it longer than a quarter of an hour. Then we had to use a cold water shower again to get rid of the sulphur. I have never been more clean in my life, having four ablutions in a single hour! Throughout the trip I had the companionship of jovial Reverend John Waldron, minister of the Holmdel Community Church on the New Jersey seashore—a great boon in itself.

CONTINUED TEACHING AND RESEARCH

My third consolation on retirement was that my teaching responsibilities would not come to an abrupt end. Further, the fact that it would be only part-time teaching would give the opportunity for which I had been longing for years—to paint in acrylics for hours upon end. While I had a greater admiration for oil paintings because of their depth, vividness, and translucency, I was too impatient to wait days for each layer of paint to dry.

The second great advantage acrylics have over oils was that if you make a mistake you can quickly paint it out. But the main thing was to have hours and hours in which to paint for the activity was totally absorbing.

My association with Princeton Theological Seminary was a long one. It began in 1962, continued for some years at three year intervals, and finally became biennial and terminated in 1990. It was at the invitation of President James I. McCord and of Professor Donald Macleod, their expert in Homiletics. On Dr. Macleod's retirement, the invitation was renewed by his successor, Professor Thomas Long, an unusually impressive preacher himself, who had taken my historical course when studying for the doctorate. This course, labelled "Comparative Liturgics", was important to me for two reasons. One was that a course in liturgics, no matter how ecumenical its range and spirit, is hardly appropriate in a university department of Religion, but essential in a theological seminary, and especially valuable in a Protestant seminary where so much stress is laid on preaching so that worship tends to be neglected. So I was able to keep up my liturgical interests and writings in connection with this course, which dealt with Roman Catholic, Orthodox, and the varieties of Protestant worship both ancient and modern. It had the further advantage of the seminary inviting me regularly to teach returning ministers in their Summer School. This opportunity allowed me to teach the history of preaching in the English-speaking world, the correlation of theology and modern novels, and a study of modern art and church architecture.

Three books I wrote were born of these interests. These were *A Mirror of the Ministry in Modern Novels,* which was published by the Oxford University Press of New York. It contained sketches of preachers and evangelists in the novels of Hawthorne, Sinclair Lewis, and James Street. Then it analyzed divines in doubt reflected in the novels of William Hale White, Mrs. Humphry Ward, and Harold Frederick. Next came a study of Roman Catholic priests described by Georges Bernanos, François Mauriac, and Graham Greene, followed by a study of missionaries as mirrored in the novels of Somerset Maugham, A. J. Cronin, and Alan Paton. The next chapter depicted community leaders as seen in the novels of Hartzell Spence, James Gould Cozzens, and Peter De Vries, and the final chapter was an evaluation of these portraits which I entitled, "A Study in Clerical Gray."

My other book which arose in part from summer teaching was *Varieties of English Preaching 1900-1960* which was published in 1963 by the S.C.M. Press in London and Prentice-Hall, Inc. of Englewood Cliffs, New Jersey.

My teaching at Drew University, forty-two miles to the north of Princeton in Madison, New Jersey, began in 1978 as member of a triumvirate of liturgical scholars, Bard Thompson, Howard Hageman, and myself. Bard was the erudite Dean of the Graduate School at Drew who had taught Church history at Vanderbilt and Emory Universities, and Howard was the president of the oldest Protestant theological Seminary in the U. S. A., that of the Dutch Reformed Church located on the campus of Rutgers Universi-

ty in New Brunswick, New Jersey. Howard had graduated
as the top student at Harvard and lectured without a note.
Bard Thompson was widely known for his admirable book,
Liturgies of the Western Church which consisted of a series
of important historical liturgies with brief, concentrated in-
troductions to them, and a list in each case of bibliographi-
cal suggestions. So successful was this volume published
first by The World Publishing Company in its Meridian
Books division in 1962, that it went into nine printings,
when it was issued by Fortress Press of Philadelphia in
1990. I had used it regularly in my "Comparative Liturgies"
course at Princeton Seminary. I had also worked with Bard
Thompson in the Liturgical Commission of the United
Church of Christ, so I looked forward to collaborating with
him, as also with Howard Hageman. The latter had given
the renowned Stone Lectures at Princeton Theological
Seminary in 1960 which were published in 1962 by the
John Knox Press of Richmond, Virginia with the title, *Pulpit and Table: some Chapters in the History of the Worship
of the Reformed Church*. Strangely enough I had met Howard Hageman as co-lecturer in the Pennsylvania Church
College at Ursinus in my first summer at Princeton. Howard Hageman had the unusual distinction of being knight-
ed by the Queen of Holland for his contribution to Dutch
Scholarship.

It was the conviction of the three of us that a Ph.D.
in Liturgics was desperately needed by the Protestant
Churches of the United States because of the over-emphasis
on Homiletics and the neglect of Liturgics, and we felt it
important that this be taught at a Graduate School in a com-
pletely cooperative ecumenical program. The only other
comparable program was at the University of Notre Dame,
at South Bend in Indiana which understandably emphasized
Catholicism. The great advantage for our purpose was that
we had Roman Catholic experts in liturgy next door to
Madison in Morristown, with Father Gabriel Coless of the
Benedictine Abbey who had taken his doctorate at San An-
selmo in Rome, and Father Charles Gusmer who taught li-

turgical theology at Fairleigh Dickinson University also in Morristown. In later days we were able to count on other liturgical experts such as Professors Thomas Talley of General Theological Seminary in New York City, an Episcopalian, Erik Routley the eminent hymnologist who'd been my colleague on the faculty of Mansfield College, Oxford, and later joined Westminster Choir College at Princeton. We also, on Erik's lamented death, had his successor, Professor Robin Leaver, whose doctoral studies were completed at Gröningen in Holland. Finally, we could also count on the historical and theological expertise of Professor John Meyendorff representing the Orthodox Churches.

The original triumvirate of us met regularly for planning at the Bedminster Inn. Unhappily for all of us Dean Thompson died suddenly at 62 in 1987. His memorial is the success of the project and his edition of *A Bibliography of Christian Worship* was published jointly by the American Theological Library Association and the Scarecrow Press of Metuchen and London in 1989. The lion's share of this volume of 786 pages was Bard's but he was assisted by the Series Editor, Professor Kenneth Rowe, and by Professors James Pain, Gabriel Coless, Erik Routley, Charles Gusmer, Howard Hageman, and myself.

It has been my privilege to teach in this liturgical program each year since it began. The seminars that I directed at Drew included "The Origins of Anglican, Puritan, and Methodist Worship" which was popular with the several Methodist men and women in a university founded by Methodists. Other seminars were "English and American Puritanism Compared," "The Modern Liturgical Movement in Europe and North America," "The History of Christian Worship: Catholic, Orthodox, and Protestant," "Christian Initiation," and "Christian Images in Western Art." I still find the experience stimulating because the students are bright and eager. The recent results of this stimulus can be found in two books written in recent years, but in another institution.

This is the Center of Theological Inquiry in Princeton, which is on Stockton Street, and conveniently located next to Speer Library of Princeton Seminary. This was the brainchild of President McCord, who founded and directed it after his retirement from the Seminary. The attractive brick, Georgian Style building was provided by the Henry Luce Foundation commemorating the founder of the magazines *Time* and *Life*, whose father had been a Presbyterian missionary in China. It provides accommodation in elegant studies for twelve post-doctoral researchers and, after Dr. McCord's death, was first directed by Professor Daniel Hardy, formerly a teacher of theology in Birmingham and Durham Universities, who is an American Episcopalian, a deeply meditative man, and thoroughly ecumenical in outlook. Members are limited to three years maximum time for research.

While at the Center I wrote three books. One was on the theological doctrine of Divine Providence, entitled *The Vigilant God: Providence in the Thought of Augustine, Aquinas, Calvin, and Barth* published in 1992 by Peter Lang, Inc. of Berne and New York and two liturgical volumes. One was *The Worship of the American Puritans, 1629-1730*, published by Peter Lang in 1991. This had separate chapters devoted to the Beginnings, the Theology of Worship, The Calendar, Sermons, Praises, Prayers, The Sacraments, Marriages and Funerals, Ordinations and Architecture. The Conclusion included a comparison between English and American Puritan Worship. I felt the wheel had come full circle from my doctoral dissertation on *The Worship of the English Puritans* completed in 1943 (but published in 1948) and the present volume completed 48 years later.

The other liturgical volume was published by Eerdmans of Grand Rapids, Michigan and its title was *Bread off Life and Cup of Joy: Newer Ecumenical Perspectives on the Eucharist*. Since Vatican II more than a thousand liturgies have been developed by the Churches of the world and it was time to analyze the most influential of them. My book examined these Eucharists from several different

standpoints: as memorial, thanksgiving, sacrifice, eschato-
logical banquet, joyful meal of unity, mystery, liberation
and social justice, as transignification and its signs and
symbols, with a final chapter on many agreements and one
serious disagreement. It appeared in 1993.

PAINTING AND EXHIBITING

The reader may be wondering where the retirement
came in? The answer is that from 1984 to 1987 as well as
after 1992 I had ample time to devote to painting and I had
three exhibitions of my art in Princeton in 1987, 1988 and
1992.

It must appear surprising that I should have had any
exhibitions of my paintings since I have taken lessons in no
art school or university in art and only one set of evening
classes taught by Peter Smith in West Windsor High
School. I don't know whether it was my naiveté, violent
colors, or choice of unusual subjects that attracted my first
and continuing sponsor, Mrs. Arlene Smith, the Senior art
Teacher at the Princeton Day School, and she was too po-
lite to tell me why. But, at the invitation of my wife Marie-
Hélène, Arlene came to our house to a party, looked at the
paintings on the walls, and asked if she might look at the
walls in the other rooms. I readily complied. She offered
only two pieces of advice: "Don't take any lessons or it will
spoil your style" and "Use larger paper or canvas board."
She offered me my first exhibition at the Anne Reid Gallery at the Princeton Day School in 1977 and a later one in
1992. I shall always be profoundly grateful to her.

As a church historian I had always been attracted by
the vertical and soaring medieval cathedrals, and they became my first subjects. I knew that the sober grays and
browns of the exteriors and especially the interior stone-
work had in earlier days been gloriously colored by painting on the half-domes with their sculptures and murals. I
also liked to juxtapose the outside and inside of cathedrals

with my imagination of their erstwhile colors. The outsides of cathedrals were their faces towards the world, the interiors were their faces towards God, the Creator of all light and all color, whom they worshipped.

In this way I depicted some major English cathedrals, of which the most successful paintings were those of Ely, Salisbury, Durham, Norwich, Westminster Abbey, and the modern cathedrals of Liverpool (both Anglican and Roman Catholic), Coventry and Westminster Cathedral. Of the European cathedrals my best paintings were of Amiens, Paris (Notre Dame), Laon, Strasbourg, and Rheims. I also painted some of the Romanesque Abbeys, such as those in Moissac and Souillac, both with their striking sculptures of prophets, and singing half-domes. Of the modern cathedrals I enjoyed painting Coventry best, because of its celebration of the works of living English painters and sculptors, including John Piper, Graham Sutherland and Sir Jacob Epstein. It was also intriguing to try out a pointillist style in reproducing the remarkable Russian Orthodox Cathedral in Nice. I was also attracted to the Cathedral of Cologne, St John's Abbey in Minnesota, and St Patrick's Cathedral in New York City.

In that first exhibition I also included some Oxford and Cambridge College Chapels and scenes from the Princeton University campus, including its neo-Gothic Chapel, and views seen through each side of Henry Moore's large O-shaped sculpture in bronze. Estelle Sinclair in a review of the exhibition's 93 paintings, refers to the "unshaded colors of an earlier world in which red leaped forward and lapis blue receded" and called them "radiant naif paintings of Christendom's holiest sites." The single word "naif" was her undisguised opinion. A year later I also exhibited at the Princeton University league in which I added flower paintings.

In my second exhibition at the Anne Reid gallery, the critics seem to be kinder in their evaluations. The title of the show was "Paris, Palermo, and Vermont." Vermont has few buildings of any interest for me because of their Puritan lack of color but it enabled me to paint a large number of flowers, with abstractions and variegated tree leaves in their corners or in a panel below. Palermo was empha- sized because of a short holiday spent there and elsewhere in Sicily in Easter of 1990 where the mosaics of the cathe- drals and the stunning images of Christ the Pantocrator (as at Monreale and Cefalu), sent me back to pointillism again. Paris provided the great museums that stimulated me, and I had an intriguing visit to Brittany, where at Pont-Aven I saw the places where Paul Gauguin had received inspira- tion for his Yellow Christ and his Green Christ, from a church in the first example and a sculptured outdoor cal- vary in the second example. So I copied the Christ pictures and the sources of their inspiration. I was also impressed by the great castle at Josselin where Anne of Brittany is bur- ied, who was twice Queen of France. Here she and her first husband the Constable of France are buried, and this I also painted.

But the real excitement of the trip was in Sicily where the convergence of Greek, Roman, Byzantine, Mos- lem, and Norman civilizations produced the marvelous medieval cathedrals, some of which I tried to represent. Of the exhibition as a whole the Princeton "Town Topics" art editor, Marian Burdick wrote: "Although the late-blooming artist is self-taught, overall the paintings display a remarka- ble intelligence in color harmony, spatial relationships, and draftsmanship. He has even plunged unafraid into experi- menting with an amazing number of styles, from pointil- lism (with its similarity to mediaeval mosaics) to Matisse- like still lifes."

A more critical review, with some appreciation, was provided by Carlton Wilkinson in "The Trenton Times." He began: "walking into the gallery, the immediate impression is one of joy. Davies is joyful in his creative geometric di- visions of the canvas, in his bright, jumping Mediterranean colors, in his celebration of medieval ecstasy. Taken as a group his paintings make you want to laugh out loud for pleasure at the variety and dedication of his imagination." He felt that the best works were medieval in subject and style of execution. He was greatly disappointed with the flowers, and he felt that I did not have the necessary technical skills for several of my subjects. At least he was kind enough to title his article "Spirited Efforts of Horton Davies."

Other citics had been amused by the whimsicality in two paintings. After juxtaposing the inside and outside of Siena Cathedral which was so strikingly repetitive in its brown and white parallel lines, I completed the work with three contented zebras against the front steps. In another painting of dominant yellows, browns and blacks, which I titled "Tigerlilies or Leopard-Lilies?" I depicted the heads of a tiger and a leopard below three large Tiger Lilies. I am glad that at least one critic felt that I enjoyed painting and communicated that joy. No one is, of course, untaught. For over sixty years I had been visiting and analysing in art museums and galleries in Europe, South Africa, and North America. I am only too willing to recognize that my bold patterns and colors owe much to the paintings of Rouault, Van Gogh, and Matisse, nor should I forget the great pointillists, Seurat and Signac. I have probably been influenced by many other painters whose impact I do not recognize. I am an amateur in the sense of being a nonprofessional, but also in the literal meaning of this borrowed French word, a "lover" of art, too, an enthusiast.

CONCLUSION

As I look back on a long and privileged life, crowded with memories of good parents, affectionate members of my family and friends, and helpful colleagues on three continents, and consider the different positions I have held, as pastor of a South London Congregational Church, founding Professor and Dean of Divinity at Rhodes University, Senior lecturer in Church History at Oxford, Putnam Professor of Religion at Princeton University, and finally Painter in retirement, what is the tie that binds them together? The simple answer is Christianity.

All the thirty books I have written reflect on the history of the Christian church and often on its many denominations, lamenting the past differences and enmity between them, and rejoicing in their ecumenical coming together in the present century. I have analyzed both formal and informal worship, as contrasted forms of response to the revelation of the living God expressed in both Word and Sacrament, Architecture and Hymnody, in Preaching, in Prayer and in Praise.

When retirement granted me leisure for painting, I first depicted the historical cathedrals of Europe, linking their exteriors and interiors with vivid and joyful colors to express the gratitude and reverence of the worshippers. In contrast, I also delineated the simpler dignity of the Puritan Churches in New England and the historic devotion of Jewish Synagogues. My next phase of painting expressed my joy in the creation, rarely in landscapes, but frequently in the rich variety and vivid splendor of flowers. More recently, I have represented the central events of Christianity, the Crucifixion and the Resurrection of Christ, proofs of the

sacrificial love of the Incarnate Son of God, and the Eternal
Father's vindication of Him, which are fundamental sources
of faith, compassion and hope in this life and the next.

My odyssey without the direction of the Christian
faith would have been merely pointless wandering from
Europe to Africa and North America. As I look back, its
purpose has been to mirror, however inadequately, the
Light of the World, the Source of all my contentment and
profound gratitude.